U-BOAT
COMBAT MISSIONS

U-BOAT
COMBAT MISSIONS

THE PURSUERS & THE PURSUED: FIRST-HAND ACCOUNTS OF U-BOAT LIFE AND OPERATIONS

LAWRENCE PATERSON

FOREWORD BY JAK P. MALLMANN SHOWELL

BARNES & NOBLE

NEW YORK

Editorial Director: **Will Steeds**
Project Editor: **Laura Ward**
Designer: **Philip Clucas** MCSD
Photographer: **Neil Sutherland**
Production: **Robert Paulley**
Color reproduction: **Modern Age Repro House Ltd**, Hong Kong

Elephant Book Company and the author particularly wish to thank the
following for their help in preparing this book: Horst Bredow of the
Deutsches U-Boot-Museum, Cuxhaven-Altenbruch, Germany; Dieter W.
Seidler of the Deutscher Marinebund e. V, Archiv Laboe, Laboe, Germany;
Jak P. Mallmann Showell; Eric-Jan Bakker; Steve Hoxa; Jürgen Weber and
the München Ubootskameradschaft, and the many veterans who have
given the author countless hours of their time.

ISBN-13: 978-0-7607-8936-0
ISBN-10: 0-7607-8936-3

Printed and bound in China

10 9 8 7 6 5 4 3 2 1

Jacket and front cover illustration: *U-47 at Scapa Flow* by Donald O'Brien,
ISMP (website: www.ismpart.com/obrien.html)

Contents

Foreword

This book is not about the war, but about the people who were imprisoned by it. They were imprisoned in "Iron Coffins" by their deep-seated conviction to do their duty for their country.

A few of these ordinary men became international heroes, but the majority remained in obscurity; living, working, and fighting under the most torturous conditions humanity has ever devised.

The people in this book are not described in the hyperbolic language of some historians but in their own words—many of them spoke in a foreign language. Yet, despite their struggling with the awkwardness of unfamiliar words, these individuals have provided a far more pertinent and more deeply horrifying picture than any of the meaningless stone epitaphs which litter much of Europe.

For every U-boat man who survived, there were three more who could no longer speak for themselves because they were swallowed by the watery graves of World War II. So, it is important that the few who remain tell following generations how pitifully people were treated by war.

Konteradmiral Eberhard Godt, Chief of the U-boat Arm's Operations Department, once said, "With some things I do not know whether I remember them, whether I dreamed about it, whether my imagination played a role or whether someone told me." This problem has hardly been recognized by modern gatherers of history, and the media bombards us with an incredible volume of self-fabricated stories. No one, not even this book, is immune from such duplicity. But naval history stands out because both sides kept diaries at the time when events took place, and therefore it is possible to check statements made by sailors. When one does this, one comes to the astounding conclusion that the voices recorded in this book are not speaking for themselves, but for all soldiers, of all nations, of all times.

Jak P. Mallmann Showell
Folkestone, England, January 2007

Introduction

Twice during the turbulent years of the 20th century, German U-boats forged a reputation for aggressive action at sea. During World War I, U-boats came to be recognized as a potentially decisive weapon, capable of sapping their enemies' will and ability to fight by attacking not only their warships but also their vital merchant supply routes. Three decades later, as World War II began, U-boats were once again seen to be operating with an almost unparalleled aggression and determination. For, on the day that Britain and France declared war on Germany—September 3, 1939—a passenger liner was torpedoed in a tragic case of mistaken identity. The established image of the U-boat man was thus reinforced and perpetuated.

During the early months of World War II, Britain became increasingly isolated as Nazi Germany swept victoriously through Western Europe, and once again merchant convoys, particularly those from North America, became crucial to the survival of the embattled island nation. What has now become famous as The Battle of The Atlantic began—and it was to cost the lives of thousands of men on both sides of the conflict.

Both over the course of the Battle and subsequently, and in the popular imagination at least, the *Kriegsmarine*'s U-boat service—along with the men who served in it—were demonized as ruthless and cold-blooded instruments of the Nazi war machine. This book looks beneath the stereotype to give a different picture. It shows that these were ordinary men who, in the main, were no more politically driven than the recruits to the armed services of any other nation. They had joined what was perceived as an elite service, the cream of a resurgent Germany's navy and, over the course of the War, three quarters of them—no fewer than 30,000 men—would die.

This book is an opportunity to allow some of those who survived to tell of their experiences. I have collected the accounts that feature here from interviews conducted over many years, and from letters and other archive sources. Now, more than 60 years after the end of the War, many of these men are no longer with us, but their words offer unique insights into the human cost of the War. Journalists and writers often refer to the "horrors" of war. Here, whether the accounts are from ordinary seamen, captains, or staff officers, the true picture that emerges—despite the frequent flashes of humor—is of the particular horrors of warfare as experienced by the men of the *Kriegsmarine*'s U-boat service in their aptly named "Iron Coffins."

Lawrence Paterson,
Thorpe Mandeville, England, March 2007

PART 1
History and Development

Preparing for a War Patrol

History and Development

The image of Hitler's "Grey Wolves" —as the U-boats were popularly known—stalking the seas for their unwary quarry of merchantmen has been etched onto the minds of successive generations since World War II. And yet the genesis of this awesome naval force can be traced back to the earlier, bitter conflicts of World War I, by the end of which, in November 1918, the U-boat had proved itself to be the most fearsome weapon in the Imperial German and Austrian Navy's formidable arsenal.

Over the course of the war, Germany's undersea warriors had inflicted repeated blows on Britain's Royal Navy and her merchant fleets, which struggled to keep the island nation supplied during the long years of attrition. The only means by which Germany had stood any chance of cutting supplies to Britain was through a successful submarine blockade. During 1917, their endeavors came perilously close to success.

With the end of World War I, the victors were determined to prevent Germany from developing submarines for use in any future conflict: the harsh terms of the Treaty of Versailles, which was signed in 1919, specifically forbade the construction of U-boats for whatever skeletal navy a defeated Germany might be allowed to possess. Despite this, Germany's military strategists were determined to remain abreast of developments in underwater warfare systems—even well before Hitler's assumption of power in 1933.

During 1922 Admiral Paul Behncke, commander-in-chief of the *Reichsmarine*, Germany's postwar navy, had authorized covert construction of a new generation of U-boats. Germany secretly financed design work by 30 engineers, many of whom had been seconded from the armaments company, Krupp; this task force was controlled by board members of three German shipbuilding yards. Later, under cover of a Dutch firm— Ingenieurskantoor voor Scheepsbouw (IvS), which was registered in The Hague—submarine design and construction began in Spain and Finland. Former chief of construction at the powerful Germaniawerft shipyard,

Previous page: Type IIAs, the first generation of Kriegsmarine U-boats, pictured in prewar calm. Left: The classic lines of a Type VIIC, which formed the backbone of the U-boat service.

Doctor of Engineering Hans Techel headed the company, while retired naval officer *Korvkpt* Ulrich Blum held the post of technical director.

During 1925 German Naval Ministry funds were put into IvS development and an order was also obtained from Turkey for two U-boats, to be designed by IvS but built in Turkey. In addition there was the tantalizing prospect of building U-boats for Spain. *Korvkpt* Wilhelm Canaris, who would later form and head the German Military Secret Service (the *Abwehr*) was dispatched to Spain to negotiate the supply of armaments and, shortly afterward, he ordered the establishment of a dedicated submarine office under the nomenclature "Au" (*Ausbildung*— Training), which would be commanded by Admiral Arno Spindler. *Au* subsequently completed prototype designs for three different submarines: one small 250-ton vessel, one medium 500-ton vessel, and a 750-ton large model. Three of the small types, designated *Vesikkos*, and three of the mediums, *Vetehinens*, were constructed in Finland, while a single large submarine, *E1*, and all initial torpedoes and torpedo tubes were built in Spain. In 1928, a new and more convenient cover firm was established—the Berlin-based Ingenieurbüro für Wirtschaft und Technik GmbH (Igewit). Under Igewit the fledgling U-boat arm slowly began to take shape in earnest. Although shipbuilders in the host countries continued to manufacture the boats, working from plans supplied by the *Reichsmarine*/IvS design teams, the knowledge was German; and the experience gained in construction and design techniques would prove invaluable in the future.

Spindler also needed a team of seamen and engineering officers to take part in the testing of the two submarines that had been designed for the Turkish Navy. German Naval Command considered that for political reasons—involvement in submarine development was a flagrant violation

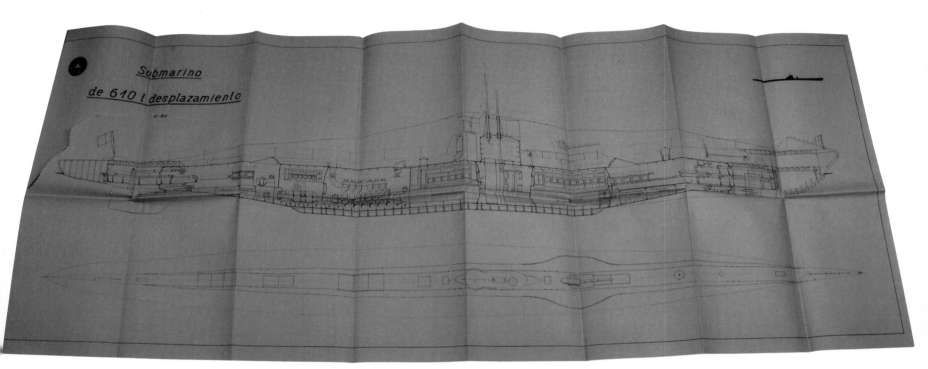

Above: *Construction plan from the IvS shipyard, one of several "front" companies for German U-boat development in the interwar period.*

of the Versailles Treaty terms—only retired military personnel should be employed, together with a small, though highly experienced civilian staff. Two of the retired German officers involved were asked to establish a U-boat training school for Turkish, and of course German, crews.

Spindler was active in establishing a training program in Germany, too, during this time; in conjunction with the Navy Arms Superintendent, he set up a series of theoretical lectures on U-boat seamanship and warfare for senior Ensigns. These began in 1927 and were included in the Ensign's torpedo courses at the newly created "Torpedo and Radio School" in Flensburg-Mürwik. The training aids used to introduce the pupils to the principles of underwater warfare included movies taken during World War I aboard *U35* and *U139*. On the engineering side, Spindler planned a training program for future U-boat men, to be introduced from 1927 onward. Trainees were encouraged to come up with ideas of how both to preserve and develop the knowledge and experience gained during World War I by the Kaiser's U-boat men.

The full U-boat training program was finally initiated under the guise of the course for 60 naval Ensigns, which was given at the Marine Artillery School at Kiel, Germany, during the early part of 1929. *Kpt z S* Hans Schottky, a former lecturer, replaced Spindler in the U-boat Office in the second half of 1929. Schottky made great efforts to implement simulator training for Ensigns. His ideas were not, however, adopted by the Naval Ministry as they were deemed to be logistically impractical. Despite this setback for U-boat training development, Schottky and a mixed group of serving officers, retired officers, civilian engineers, and sundry officials managed to gain practical experience during the testing of the two now-completed Finnish boats *Vetehinen (CV-702)* and *Vesihiisi (CV-703)* at the small port of Turku in Finland in the summer of 1930.

By 1931, despite certain difficulties, the Spanish boat *E1* had also been completed. This large submarine had been launched on October 22 the previous year, but had promptly run aground after hitting the water. *E1* was to be studied by German designers as the possible prototype "backbone" for Germany's future submarine force (*UA* and two Type IA boats were the result). *Kptlt* Robert Bräutigam was head of the German testing team. For some years Bräutigam had been in charge of Japan's submarine construction, all of which was similarly based on German design work.

During 1933 German defense minister General Werner von Blomberg ordered the establishment of a fully-fledged submarine school in Kiel-Wik (Wik is a suburb of Kiel). *Kptlt* Slevogt was appointed Commanding Officer, with Senior Lecturers Fürbringer and Hülsmann, and Junior

Above: *Karl Dönitz and Albert Speer (left), architect and armaments minister from 1942.*

Lecturers Rösing and Freiwald. On June 25, 1933, the school's first course began. The school's inaugural "crew" (each year's class was designated a "crew") comprised eight officers, and nearly 80 NCOs and seamen.

The training establishment's official title was the "Anti-Submarine School" (*Unterseebootsabwehrschule*, or *UAS*), and it was technically incorporated into the Torpedo Inspectorate. Theoretical training included lessons in U-boat construction from the point of view of both sailor and engineer, instruction in maintaining stability, weight distribution, and trim above and below water, during both peacetime and war conditions, and the use of escape apparatus. Men of the seamen branch received basic training in torpedo firing, and officers and senior ratings in the use of the periscope. Engineering personnel, meanwhile, were taught the mechanics and theory of both diesel and electric propulsion units. Hardware used during the intensive courses included an electrically operated steering machine, as well as an electric periscope and gyrocompass installation.

were sent to Finland disguised as tourists and students.

Meanwhile, in the mid-1930s, Germany had begun constructing U-boat components on her native soil—by November 1934 component frames for 12 U-boats had been completed in the Ruhr. Copied directly from tried-and-tested designs developed by IvS, they were transferred to Kiel in the utmost secrecy, where they were stored in warehouses at the Germaniawerft and Deutsche Werke shipyards during January 1935. The diesel and electric engines followed, and then the torpedo-tube armament. In June 1935 the first of Germany's new U-boats, the small Type IIA coastal submarine *U1*, commanded by *Kptlt* Klaus Ewerth, was launched at the Deutsche Werke shipyard.

Above: *The daily chores of a Kriegsmarine recruit mirrored those of naval servicemen worldwide. Here, mattresses are given a morning airing.*

Practical training was carried out initially with the aid of primitive, though ingenious, simulators. These comprised elderly minesweepers equipped with a periscope stub housed within a covered deck compartment. An engine installation consisting of half of a Type II drive unit, with submarine steering equipment, completed the simulation. Training took place aboard these minesweepers and aboard *CV707* in Finland between May and August 1935. To take part in the Finnish exercises seven officers and six NCOs

With Germany's submarine development activities now effectively in the open, Adolf Hitler's March 16, 1935, formal announcement that Germany would rearm—Army conscription would be introduced, the *Luftwaffe* would be established, and new German battleships constructed—came as no surprise. Although with this declaration Hitler was effectively tearing up the Versailles Treaty, pursuing its policy of appeasement Britain nevertheless signed a Naval Agreement with Germany in London on June 18, 1935,

Above right: *Training on a U-boat planesmen position simulator. Submariner training was intense, even before the actual U-boats were ready.*
Above left: *Trainees at Flensburg–Mürwik, the radiotelegraphy school founded in 1902.*

which allowed Germany to develop a *Kriegsmarine* 35 per cent the size of the Royal Navy and a submarine arm 45 per cent of the size of Britain's—with a clause allowing up to 100 per cent with the vague insistence of "due notification." Although a further "Submarine Protocol" was signed by Germany's foreign minister, Joachim von Ribbentrop in 1936, proposing the outlawing of the submarine as a weapon of war, and pledging that Germany would never again resort to unrestricted submarine warfare, Germany had effectively been granted permission to develop its U-boat arm openly.

The strategic framework that would dictate the U-boat service's subsequent expansion was simple: *Generaladmiral* Erich Raeder, supreme commander-in-chief of the *Kriegsmarine*, wanted a force capable of striking at the arteries of trade that would be essential to the survival of its likely enemies, Britain and France, in any conflict. He also wished to avoid any direct and prolonged clash with the Royal Navy—the most powerful navy in the world—which he believed would end in the inevitable destruction of the *Kriegsmarine* (in World War I Germany's great surface ships of the High Seas Fleet had remained bottled-up in harbor, apart from one or two forays into the North Sea). The U-boat service would enable the *Kriegsmarine* to disrupt lines of supply—and, in theory, to slip away, undetected by the ships of the world's most powerful navy.

The centrality of the U-boat service to Raeder's strategic thinking led to its rapid development. The launching of *U1* in June 1935 had heralded the formation of a new training unit, the *Unterseebootsschulflottille* (U-boat School Flotilla), which soon comprised *U1* to *U6* as further boats were launched. This then came under the jurisdiction of the Torpedo Inspectorate. The first "operational" U-boat flotilla, made up of Type IIB boats, was commissioned by *Fregkpt* Karl Dönitz during September 1935, and shortly afterward he was promoted to full captain with the rank of *Kapitän zur See*. At this stage Dönitz was a flotilla commander and did not receive the new title of Flag Officer for U-boats (*Führer der Unterseeboote*) until the following January.

Dönitz had begun his own naval career in Germany's Imperial Navy in April 1910, serving initially as an officer on the cruiser SMS *Breslau*. Based mainly in Istanbul, SMS *Breslau* and SMS *Goeben* were a constant presence in the Dardanelles area during World War I; they were handed over to the Turks and were then crewed by men of both nations. When they emerged from the Dardanelles Straits and headed for the Aegean on January 20, 1918, both ships were opposed by British destroyers and monitors. They evaded the British, but struck mines off Imbros, *Breslau* sinking immediately while *Goeben*, badly holed, was beached in the Dardanelles Narrows (which lead into the Straits). Meanwhile, in October 1916 Dönitz had transferred to U-boats. Initially he served as First Watch Officer aboard *U39* (for five patrols), before rising to command the minelayer *UC25* (two patrols), and then *UB68* (one patrol) with the rank of *Oberleutnant zur See*.

Above: *The white Mütze (cap) of a rating belonging to the "Saltzwedel" Flotilla (renamed the 2nd U-Flotilla in 1940). Identifying cap bands such as this were removed following the outbreak of War.*

Below: *The officer crew of U11—part of the fledgling "Weddigen" Flotilla—pictured in 1935. From left to right: Chief Engineer Oblt (Ing.) Schmidt, Commander Kptlt Hans-Rudolf Rösing, and IWO Oblt Dietrich von der Ropp.*

Dönitz's latter command was sunk in 1918 following a catastrophic loss of longitudinal stability during an attack on British shipping in the Mediterranean. The stricken U-boat plunged out of control to 300ft (91m) before rocketing to the surface, where it lay at the mercy of Allied guns (the sinking was attributed primarily to HMS *Snapdragon*). Six men were killed and the rest of the crew, including the distraught commander, were captured. After spending nine months in a British prisoner-of-war camp Dönitz was released, and returned to a ruined Germany. Following a brief stint as a torpedo boat captain he was promoted to commission a brand-new torpedo boat half-flotilla. After holding a variety of subsequent posts he was finally made commander of the cruiser *Emden*, aboard which prospective naval officers received basic naval training during a year-long world cruise. *Emden* had been brought back into service with a brand-new crew after a refit, so this was the second time that Dönitz commissioned a brand-new unit with new men, which made him an attractive choice to launch the fledgling U-boat flotilla.

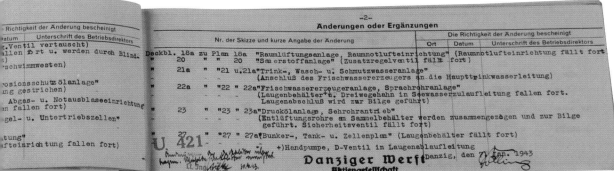

Above: *Launching a new Type VII at the Germaniawerft in Kiel. Over 700 different Type VIIs were commissioned.*
Left: *Engineer's "sketchbook," issued by the shipyard in which the boat was built, in this case the Danziger Werft from which* U421 *was launched in September 1942.*

The U-boat service's new commander-in-chief had fresh ideas on the best way to conduct U-boat warfare. Influenced by his own experiences of the difficulties involved in submarine warfare, Dönitz preached a creed of tightly organized group attacks against merchant shipping by commanders and crew trained to be aggressive and daring. The early tactics developed in Baltic Sea training urged captains to "shadow" sighted convoy traffic, signaling other boats to gather before launching a concerted attack. U-boats were to remain surfaced and use their high diesel speed and small surface silhouette to full advantage, attacking with torpedoes under the protection of darkness. Dönitz and his men knew that once submerged, the U-boat was slow and unwieldy, restricted by the limitations of its electric engines, which in turn, of course, were reliant on quickly depleted banks of batteries.

With this emphasis on attack, Dönitz frequently admonished those he

felt showed a lack of aggression, though his doctrine was tempered with genuine concern for the welfare and survival of his men. The close relationship forged in those early years between Dönitz and those under his command continued well into the hard times of World War II, when his U-boat service had grown to number hundreds of boats and thousands of men. He would personally debrief returning captains, asking pointed questions about the decisions they had made at sea, while poring over the boat's War Diary—the onboard log book that recorded everything from course changes to attack patterns. Rewards would follow for those who earned them, while men found lacking were rotated out of the U-boat service to other branches of the *Kriegsmarine*. To his men Dönitz became known as "*Der Löwe*"—The Lion—and his dynamic personality affected all aspects of U-boat operations.

Dönitz had stated that he required a force of 300 U-boats in the event of war with Britain. This would allow 100 at sea at any given time, another 100 in transit, and the last 100 in port or dockyard. At the outbreak of war against France, Britain and its Dominions on September 3, 1939, Dönitz

The most senior of the seamen was the combined navigator and quartermaster (*Obersteuermann*). Alongside him as senior non-commissioned officer, or warrant officer, rank was the bosun (*Bootsmann*) and any midshipmen (*Fähnriche zur See*) serving aboard the boat. Further down, the chain of command passed through the chief bosun's mate and bosun's mate, to the torpedo crew led by the *Torpedomechaniker*, or Torpedo Mechanic, and comprising a mixed array of enlisted men who also manned any surface weaponry aboard the boat.

The Technical Branch was headed by chief diesel and electrical machinists (*Obermaschinisten*), warrant and other petty officers, machinist and electrician's mates, and the two senior radio non-commissioned officers. Later in the War the more senior ranks of *Stabsobermaschinist* and *Stabsobersteuermann* were added, this applying to other trades as well. Enlisted men were spread between the engines, motors, hydrophone, and radio rooms. Together the two branches operated one of Germany's most successful, though ultimately flawed, weapons of war.

Left: The personal staff-car pennant for Grossadmiral Karl Dönitz, who was promoted to this rank on January 31, 1943.

Below: Germany's ambitious U-boat program—in the open by 1935—was maintained to the last days of the War.

possessed only 57 U-boats, 46 of which were combat vessels. Twenty of his front-line boats were small coastal Type IIs, clearly unsuited to the rigors of an Atlantic war. Of the remainder, two were Type Is, which, according to historians, had proved unsatisfactory in prewar trials. (Admiral Godt and *Kriegsmarine* records describe them as being "difficult to handle" rather than unsatisfactory.) Seventeen Type VIIs were also available—this being the successful medium design that Dönitz envisaged as a perfect compromise between weapon capacity, range at sea, and speed. The remaining seven combat boats were the replacement design for the unwieldy Type I, designated the Type IX.

Despite their numerical inferiority, Dönitz's men had been imbued with a high *esprit de corps*, which they carried with them into action. The crew aboard a typical combat U-boat varied in number between 25 aboard a Type II to as many as 56 aboard the large ocean-going Type IXs. The boat's officers would comprise the commander, at least an *Oberleutnant zur See* in rank, the First and Second Watch Officers, either *Oberleutnant* or *Leutnant zur See*, the chief engineer, at least an *Oberleutnant* (*Ing.*), and possibly additional officers who were in training or, later in the War, a doctor. Beneath them, whatever the number, the crew was divided into two separate branches: Seaman (*Seemann*) and Technical (*Techniker*).

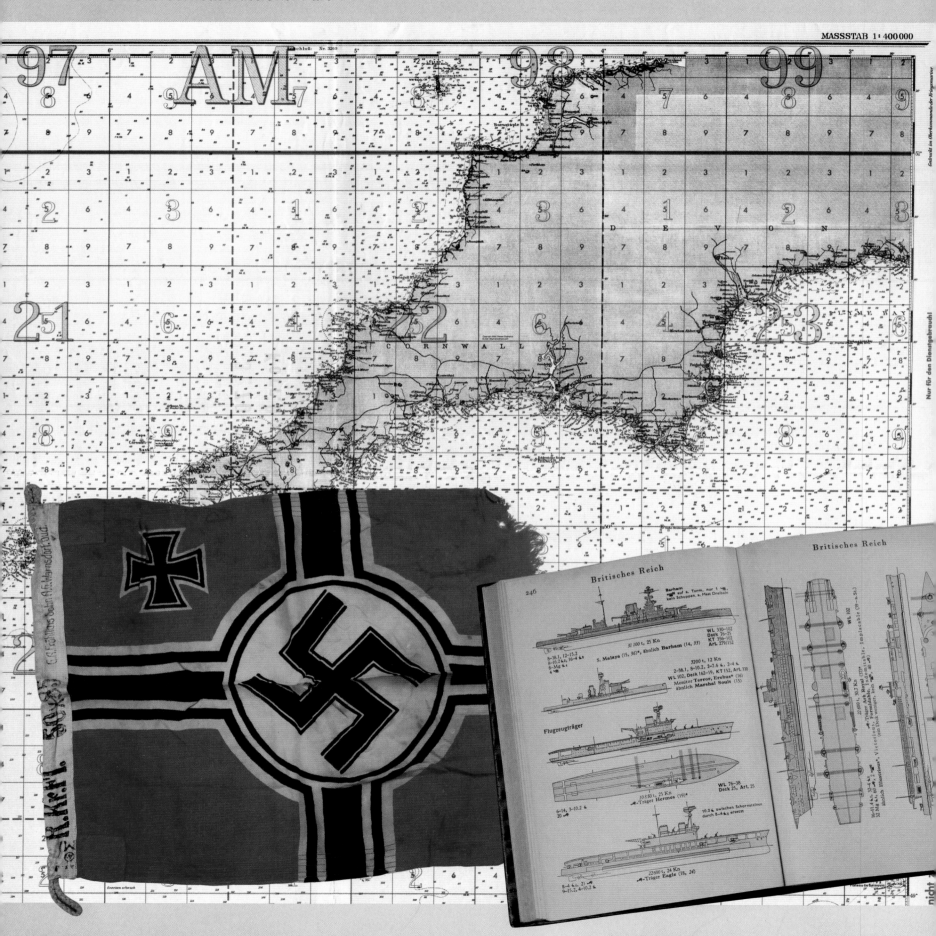

Preparing for a War Patrol

The task of preparing a U-boat for a war patrol began long before it actually departed its home port. After the rigors of its previous mission—whether a patrol or a training stint in the Baltic Sea—the boat would spend weeks in the dockyard being overhauled. The overhaul would include repainting to help protect the hull from rust and the corrosive effect of salt, any necessary repairs, and fixing any mechanical defects identified when the boat was last at sea, as well as maintenance and calibration of onboard systems. Once the overhaul was competed, both boat and crew would be put through a series of rigorous trials to insure that they were ready for combat action.

The U-boats would be tested for faults with a brief run out of harbor, including a test submergence, to detect any particular problems requiring attention. The boat would then be "depermed"—a procedure that aimed to eliminate as much magnetic trace as possible from the hull by surrounding the boat with a series of electrically charged magnetized wire loops. This would theoretically negate some of the threat from enemy minefields and also allow the boat a greater chance of avoiding aerial detectors such as the so-called Magnetic Anomaly Detectors ("MADs"). (These devices were able to detect the presence of large, submerged metallic objects by measuring fluctuations in the earth's natural magnetic field.) Once back in the dockyard the boat's final overhaul would involve whatever rust treatment was still required and the checking of systems, such as compasses, echo sounders, radars or radar detectors, and periscopes. It would now be just days before the patrol would begin.

Left: One of the unsung heroes of Germany's U-boat service, Eberhard Godt (center), head of BdU Operations Staff, is shown here with Staff Officer Victor Oehrn at his left.

Either Dönitz, his flotilla commander, or an officer from BdU would then brief the boat's captain. Each patrol would be carefully planned to insure that sufficient provisioning, armaments, and personnel were provided for the specific mission in mind. Missions ranged in type from relatively straightforward anti-shipping torpedo patrols, minelaying, or any number of special operations. The landing of agents or weather stations on remote islands within the North Atlantic and Polar seas would sometimes be undertaken as a priority assignment before the boat would be freed for action against enemy shipping.

Once the captain was aware of the nature of his boat's next mission he would in turn order the *Steuermann* (Navigator) to obtain the necessary maps and charts from the flotilla headquarters. Although no announcement would be made to the crew about their destination, speculation would become rife as soon as any glimpse of the navigator's charts was gained. The charts covered all the areas that the *Kriegsmarine* was destined to penetrate, and were divided into a series of grid squares. Each large square of 486 nautical miles each side was identified by two letters of the alphabet. That square was then divided into nine numerically designated squares, a pattern repeated three more times until a final grid square covering an approximate area of 4.25 nautical miles per side—equating to 18 square nautical miles of sea—was reached. Thus navigators ordered to proceed to grid square BF3192 would find themselves at 50°23' N 01°17' W, just south of the Isle of Wight. It was by this method of navigation that BdU would direct U-boats to far-flung areas of the ocean; the grid system also enabled tightly organized patrol lines—or, as they became more famously known, "Wolf Packs"—to be organized.

Left: A map showing Britain's southwest coast, overlaid by the Kriegsmarine's complex grid system; to the left is the tattered battle flag of U285, sunk without any survivors southwest of Ireland on April 15, 1945. A 1941/2 issue of Weyers' military identification book (bottom right).

Below: The transfer of individually cased artillery rounds from a flatbed rail car in the dockyard to an awaiting U-boat was a laborious procedure.

in the Indian Ocean and even briefly within the Pacific Ocean, during 1944. Though occasionally called upon for special duties—such as the landing of saboteurs, weather stations or to cruise as solitary raiders—the disruption of convoys was the core task of U-boat operations. Indeed the original concept behind the development of the U-boat, as stated, envisioned it primarily as being a weapon for use against merchant shipping.

Within three days of the expected departure of the boat, torpedoes, deck and Flak-gun munitions would be taken onboard. Torpedoes were lowered using a sturdy block-and-tackle arrangement combined with a purpose-designed cradle through the torpedo loading hatches at bow and stern for Type VII and IX U-boats. There, they were lowered into storage beneath the flooring of the torpedo compartments, and above the bow-room floor, where they were covered in planking that allowed the occupants of the compartment to walk on them. Also, every tube would be loaded. Type II U-boats possessed only three forward tubes, and unlike the larger boats the torpedoes were loaded aboard tailfin-first through the hatchway. On the other end of the scale, the largest combat boat used in action—the minelayer Type XB—possessed only two stern tubes. During

Above: An MP40, one of the standard-issue small arms carried aboard combat U-boats. Though deployed rarely, they were on hand for guard duty, close combat, even hunting!

Below, far left: Fuel—seen here being pumped aboard—was distributed evenly between internal and saddle tanks, giving the Type VIIC its characteristic bulges.
Below: External canisters provided increased torpedo capacity, and, on the long-distance Type IXD2 U-boats (as here, on U861), storage space.

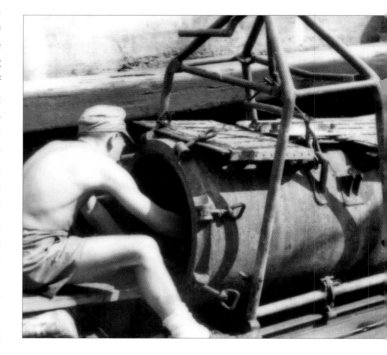

Although, when the War began, Dönitz's central theater of operations was the Atlantic Ocean with its vital convoy routes that kept Britain from starvation, his U-boats became active in every major ocean of the globe. Despite his shortage of combat boats, frequent diversions of strength to the Mediterranean, Black Sea, and the Arctic Circle were also made. Eventually U-boats became active

1945 the small coastal electro-boat—the Type XXIII—was introduced, possessing only two bow tubes; space was so cramped within the boat that they were loaded externally.

Once the boat's interior torpedoes had been stowed, whatever exterior storage available for that size of U-boat was also filled with the long deadly cylinders, held in watertight canisters located beneath the outer decking. The Type VIIC—backbone of the German U-boat service—carried a total of 14 torpedoes (including two in external canisters fore and aft); alternatively, this type could carry up to 39 mines.

The artillery rounds, both for the 88mm deck gun and whatever Flak weaponry was fitted, were taken into the hull sealed in water- and pressure-tight containers. Type VIIBs and VIICs carried about 250 rounds for the 88mm quick-firing deck gun and about 4,380 rounds of 20mm ammunition for the Flak gun or guns. (In recent years, containers salvaged from U-boat wrecks have been found to contain shells in prime condition.) The 20mm shells were stored in small magazines for clipping onto the guns. Later during the War, when the large deck guns were being removed, there was room to carry more anti-aircraft ammunition.

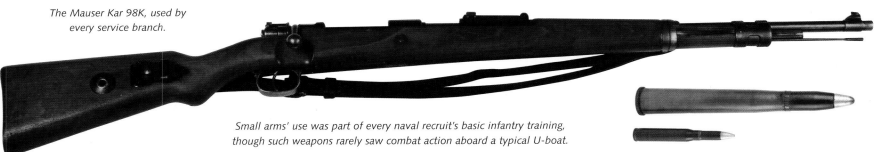

The Mauser Kar 98K, used by every service branch.

Small arms' use was part of every naval recruit's basic infantry training, though such weapons rarely saw combat action aboard a typical U-boat.

The ammunition was stored beneath the decking in the boat's magazine, which was accessed through a hatch between the captain's quarters and the radio and sound rooms. This magazine was also used to house the few small arms carried aboard a combat boat. Though the combination of such weaponry varied enormously, typically it comprised two or three Mauser 98K rifles with bayonets, a pair of MP40 submachine guns, and six Mauser pistols, and possibly also some hand grenades. Occasionally the guns were fitted in a rack within the wardroom, while the pistols were sometimes kept in a locked chest in the captain's "cabin" though, more often

than not, they were stored below deck in the magazine. (In the Black Sea—where six Type II U-boats were deployed—the small arms were used in fierce battles with Russian surface craft. That largely forgotten arena saw some of the fiercest surface-fighting undertaken by U-boats in World War II.) Toward the end of the War, U-boats often carried MG34 machine guns that could be mounted on the conning tower to provide additional anti-aircraft firepower. These were, of course, extremely vulnerable to the effects of seawater, and they required constant maintenance. They also had to be dismounted from the tower before the boat submerged.

Above: Flak ammunition. The 20mm (below) was rapid firing but of limited range, while the 37mm was more potent, but slower firing—a trade-off between firepower and speed.

Top: U37 takes on torpedoes in 1939. The flotilla commander's pennant is visible on the bridge; U37 was the only combat U-boat to fly one, under the command of Korvkpt Werner Hartmann, chief of the "Hundius" Flotilla.

tanks), but also into the actual diving tanks—the *Tauchbunker*—where it would float on the top of the denser, and thus heavier, seawater. This system was the so-called "self-compensating" fuel bunker, referring to the fact that the bunker was open to seawater at the bottom, the lighter diesel floating on top of it. As the fuel was consumed, it would be replaced in the tank by seawater. (This system prevented air bubbles from forming that could upset the boat's trim, and it also eliminated the risk of trapped air leaking to betray the U-boat's position.) Alongside these outboard fuel bunkers, the compensating tanks were designed to be partially flooded in the manner of normal ballast tanks.

Left: Kriegsmarine *stores. Large quantities of material were supplied locally to U-boat bases in occupied countries.*
Below: *A Type VIIC (left) and a Type IX (right) take on supplies. The* Schnorchel *on the Type IX's conning tower dates it to late War, while the band identifies it as a training boat.*

The day after the arming had taken place, long-lasting, conserved provisions were taken aboard. These consisted of canned goods that would form the bulk of the diet for the second part of the patrol. Everything from powdered eggs and milk to canned bread, vegetables, and fruit were hidden away in whatever space could be found for it. Heavy marine-grade diesel fuel would then be taken aboard. The fuel would be pumped into the cavernous fuel bunkers—not only into the *Regelbunker* (compensating

Once underway, the engines tended to be run on the fuel within the compensating tanks first, so that they would be returned to their dedicated purpose. Whenever fuel was taken from the free-flooding cells, it was first sent to a collecting tank and then through a purifier to eliminate any traces of water. From there it entered the "daily use" tank that dominated the ceiling of the engine room. Daily trim calculations were the domain of the chief engineer as he measured the exact amount of fuel consumed so as

onboard, while washing water came via a fire hydrant. The whole stock took at least a day to complete, supervised by the boat's IIIWO (Third Watch Officer), who was responsible for insuring not only that it was able to sustain itself at sea, but that the boat was also capable of combat, with vital systems all clearly within reach despite the crowded interior.

With the boat finally cleared for sea the crew would be transported from its barracks to the dockside, with the men's belongings being carried inside heavy canvas sea bags or suitcases. Once assembled, the crew made their own way to a flotilla office, where their bags were placed in storage. In the event that they did not return from their patrol, these bags would be sent to their families back in

Far left: *Aboard this pre-War U-boat, the eagle emblem still adorns the conning tower. It was removed following the outbreak of War, though some boats retained the plaque for several weeks afterward.*

Below left: *Stores are unloaded dockside before being carried via the gangplank to the boat. Combat preparedness was as much a matter of provisions as ammunition.*

Below right: *Each item was carefully checked off against a master list. Ultimately the responsibility of the Obersteuermann (possibly right, in shore uniform), here the Bootsmannsmaat seems to be doing the checking.*

to be able to adjust the boat's trim due to the increased amount of seawater within the tanks.

As the boat underwent its last stages of maintenance after stocking with preserved foodstuffs, the crew would also undergo their own fitness checks. The flotilla medical officer would examine each man to insure his readiness for service. Any problems would either delay sailing, or in more serious cases, require the removal of the crewman. Skin infections in particular were the bane of U-boat men. Brought on by the damp, stale atmosphere, the infections could spread rapidly among the closely confined crew, to the point where the men's combat effectiveness would be undermined.

On the final day, the fresh food—bread, fruit, vegetables, eggs, and meat—would be loaded. Sausages and hams would be hung between the forward torpedo tubes and the stern section of the control room. Bread, on the other hand, would generally be stored in the hammocks that cluttered an already crowded boat, while various smoked meats would be suspended from pipes throughout the boat. Sacks of potatoes and citrus fruits would be wedged into the engine room and bow and stern compartments—this meant that the enlisted men in the bow room were reduced to sleeping wherever they could find a space. Drinking water was also taken

Germany. It was a grimly practical routine, alongside the writing of a last will and testament before operations commenced. Belongings shed, enlisted men took little more than what could be carried in the pockets of their

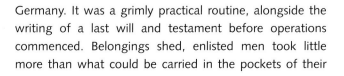

leather jackets—usually some small articles of spare clothing, or a book or writing materials, while officers were able to carry slightly more, as there was marginally more storage space in their compartment.

A final parade on deck would allow the flotilla commander, or Dönitz himself, to address the men, followed by a short speech by the boat's captain. The crew would still not know where they were headed at this stage, although if items such as arctic or tropical clothing had been stowed the men would have been able to make an educated guess as to their ultimate destination.

Finally the First Watch Officer would report the boat ready to put to sea and the men would be dismissed. This procedure altered dramatically as the War and its resultant pressures on the German Navy dragged on. Early U-boat departures were often marked with cheering crowds and military bands while the majority of the crew paraded on the boat's deck; in later years boats crept as unobtrusively as possible from their cavernous concrete bunkers, with little or no fanfare. As many of the mechanics, engineers, and laborers who worked in the dockyards were drawn from the local population (whether the port be in occupied Norway, Greece, or France), there was a very real danger that saboteurs and agents were lurking among the workers, ready to inform the enemy about U-boat movements. (Sabotage within the German dockyards became a genuine problem to the U-boat service, too.) Electric motors were generally used to ease out of harbor, lest any acoustic mines be activated by the throbbing diesels, not to mention the discomfort caused within the enclosed space of a U-boat bunker by the streams of diesel exhaust generated when the engines were fired.

Right: Karl Dönitz addresses his men; such close personal contact with their commander-in-chief inspired loyalty.

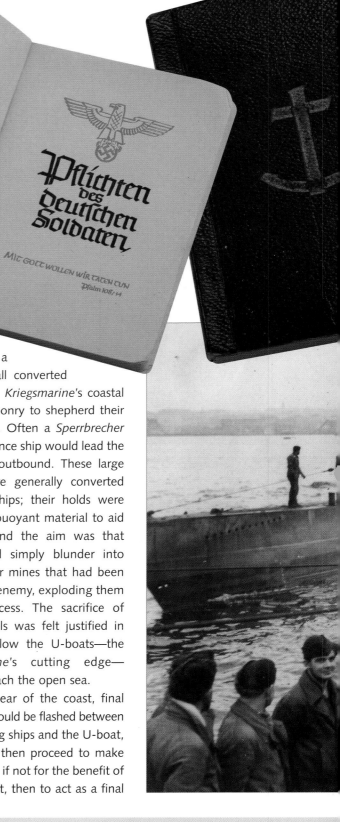

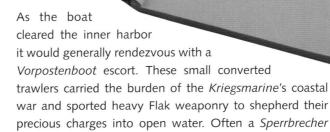

As the boat cleared the inner harbor it would generally rendezvous with a *Vorpostenboot* escort. These small converted trawlers carried the burden of the *Kriegsmarine*'s coastal war and sported heavy Flak weaponry to shepherd their precious charges into open water. Often a *Sperrbrecher* mine-clearance ship would lead the procession outbound. These large vessels were generally converted merchant ships; their holds were filled with buoyant material to aid flotation, and the aim was that they would simply blunder into any mine or mines that had been laid by the enemy, exploding them in the process. The sacrifice of these vessels was felt justified in order to allow the U-boats—the *Kriegsmarine*'s cutting edge— safely to reach the open sea.

Once clear of the coast, final messages would be flashed between the escorting ships and the U-boat, that would then proceed to make its first dive, if not for the benefit of concealment, then to act as a final test before heading into action. With all onboard systems checked, and provided there were no faults that could force a mission to be aborted, the boat would head toward its designated combat area, ready to begin its War Patrol. On the way commanders often ran through various procedures to ensure that the crew still responded sharply, and that they had not slackened off during their stay in port.

Left: *The Kriegsmarine songbook belonging to Obersteuermann* Karl Dume *of U172.*

Right and below: U604 *and* U663, *both of the 9th U-flotilla, enter Brest harbor together on the last day of 1942.*

The last night ashore

The last evening before a mission began usually featured a final run ashore for the crew. Georg Seitz remembered the celebrations in the French port of Brest before *U604* put to sea.

"We would be in the bars in town, making the most of our last bit of time ashore. Of course we were young and our comradeship was very strong so we would drink and dance with the girls and get rowdy. However I must say that we never reached the situation that you see in the popular film *Das Boot*. We never went around shooting pistols or anything like that. Also, I can't imagine ever seeing an officer so drunk that he would be unconscious and vomit on himself. We would have had no respect for such a man. So to me, that is an exaggeration and I personally don't believe it. Of course we had high spirits, but it was war and everybody did what they could to enjoy life. But nor were we gloomy and expecting the worst. Drinking and celebrating with our crew and comrades would keep us in high spirits, and then we would get back to the job that we had to do. We fought for our country and always sailed knowing that we would come back. Of course, so many didn't."

Above: Kptlt *Reinhard von Hymmen (center) and officers of U408, apparently aboard a depot ship between patrols. Von Hymmen and his crew of 44 men were killed on November 5, 1942, when U408 was sunk by depth charges. Von Hymmen had held his command for just under one year, and was on his third war patrol when his boat was sunk. He had previously served on two combat boats—U97 then U564—as a "commander in training."*

Torpedo Room and Forward Quarters

"The bow-room—bread, potatoes, and lots of people.
Life was harsh in there."—Herbert Waldschmidt, *U564*

The offensive power of the combat U-boat lay in its delivery of a torpedo payload. The Type VIIC U-boat generally possessed four bow torpedo tubes, though oddities in construction partly due to a shortage of materials at that time meant that *U72, U78, U80, U554*, and *U555* had only two forward tubes each. On the boats with four tubes, they were arranged in two banks of two, the upper pair lying slightly outboard of those below; all four protruded nearly 13ft (4m) into the bow compartment. Situated outboard of each torpedo tube were cylinders containing the compressed air that was used to launch the torpedoes. Stretching toward the end of the compartment were rails used for the loading and unloading of the tubes. Suspended by chains from the ceiling, the rails would be lowered onto the torpedoes, each of which weighed between 3,391lb (1,538kg) and 4,270lb (1,937kg), depending on the warhead fitted. Once the girders were above the torpedoes they would be fastened with strong steel bands to the 23ft (7m) long weapons, which would then be hoisted from the deck to the required height for loading. After the torpedo's guidance mechanisms and battery power (if electric) had been checked, a thick coating of grease was applied, and the torpedo would then be run into the tubes by means of hand wheels operated by the sweating crew.

Once the torpedo was inside the tube a large, free-floating greased steel piston was manually placed against

Left: *The bow room aboard U995, a single torpedo slung from its loading hoist in position at the hatch to Tube 2. It was here that the majority of the crew lived while the boat was as sea.*

the stern fins of the torpedo, and the tube shut. When the torpedo was ready to be fired, the tube would be flooded, and the outer doors opened. With the activation of the "trigger" a burst of compressed air (at approximately 24 atmospheres' pressure) pushed against the back of the piston; this propelled the torpedo free of the tube, at which point its motor activated, driving the torpedo toward its target. The piston was retained inside the tube by an ingenious arrangement that comprised a pair of grooves on opposite inner sides of the torpedo tube, into which a pair of flanges on the piston fitted. When the outer doors of the tube were open, water filled the grooves and, as the piston was propelled forward, the opposing water pressure within the groove acted against the rapidly dissipating force of the expanding air behind the piston, bringing it to a halt just before the end of the tube. A relief air valve would then automatically open at the back of the tube and water pressure would force the piston back to clang against the torpedo tube door. This process would, of course, force the air behind the piston into the boat, increasing the pressure within the hull if the boat were submerged. Once the torpedo had been launched, the outer door was closed; the water inside the tube bled into the bilge and the tube was ready to be reloaded, which generally took between 20 and 30 minutes.

Ten of the boat's 14 torpedoes were stored in the forward compartment. The four that lay within the tubes themselves had to be taken out every day and re-greased to keep them combat-ready. A further four torpedoes were stored below the floor, while the final two simply lay on top of the deck within the men's living space. These were covered with plywood sheeting, on top of which the enlisted crewmen lived and stored food. (On Type VIIs, another torpedo was stored in an external canister, above the bow compartment.) There were 12 bunks within the compartment—which had to be shared by upward of 25 men. This meant that no bunk was ever unoccupied: when one man was on duty his bunk was taken by someone else whose turn it was to rest. (The rota the men lived by kept strictly to German summer time, no matter what time zone the boat was actually in.) The interior would soon become humid and damp, regardless of the outside temperature, and the health issues associated with constant damp, a lack of sunlight and proper exercise posed frequent problems. Among the occupants were watchmen, torpedo men, engine and motor machinists (commonly referred to as "stokers," in a carry-over from times past), radio and hydrophone men, and the cook. The sole man to have a designated bunk within the compartment was the *Mechanikersmaat* (the Torpedo Petty Officer)—the only non-commissioned officer to live in the enlisted men's accommodation; his task was to maintain and operate the boat's torpedoes. As the War progressed, and as crew numbers increased (more men were needed to work the

extra equipment and Flak guns that were installed), some of these additional men had to be accommodated within the already cramped room. Usually, hammocks were strung up wherever there was space for them.

Small lockers mounted behind the bunks along the pressure hull wall gave the men a limited amount of storage space for their personal possessions. The bunks were also frequently raised to allow the stowage of extra rations or to facilitate the manhandling of torpedoes— those men not involved in the latter task would be forced to find comfort wherever they could. At the beginning of a voyage it was not uncommon for the enlisted men—the "Lords," as they were known in German naval slang—to be forced to crawl on their hands and knees to get through the compartment. However, as the patrol progressed, and as torpedoes were fired and rations consumed, valuable and much-appreciated space was released for the men to live in.

Page right, clockwise from top left: Gyro-angle receiving and setting instrument (the hand wheel was used to adjust settings on loaded torpedoes); the four bow tubes aboard U995, with the repeater for the conning tower torpedo computer located at the top, midway between the two upper tubes (note, the floor has been raised to accommodate tourists and so now encroaches on the lower tubes); twin-bladed G7e torpedo loaded in Tube 4; lamps for displaying tube readiness, illuminated when prepared to fire; the firing handle for Tube 1.

Official decorations

Awards, with service book (center), of torpedo man *Mechanikergefreiter* Josef Mock of *U281*. The U-boat Combat badge (left)—usually presented after two combat missions—and the Iron Cross, Second Class (right) were both awarded in St Nazaire on March 8, 1944, by *Kapt z S* Hans-Rudolf Rösing, FdU West.

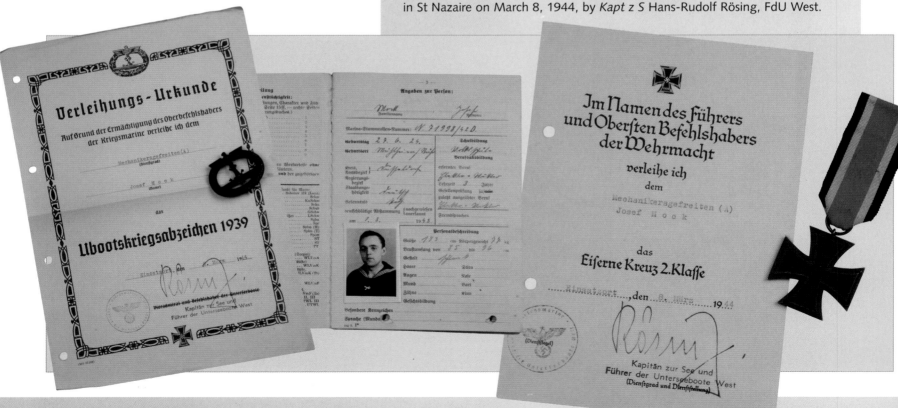

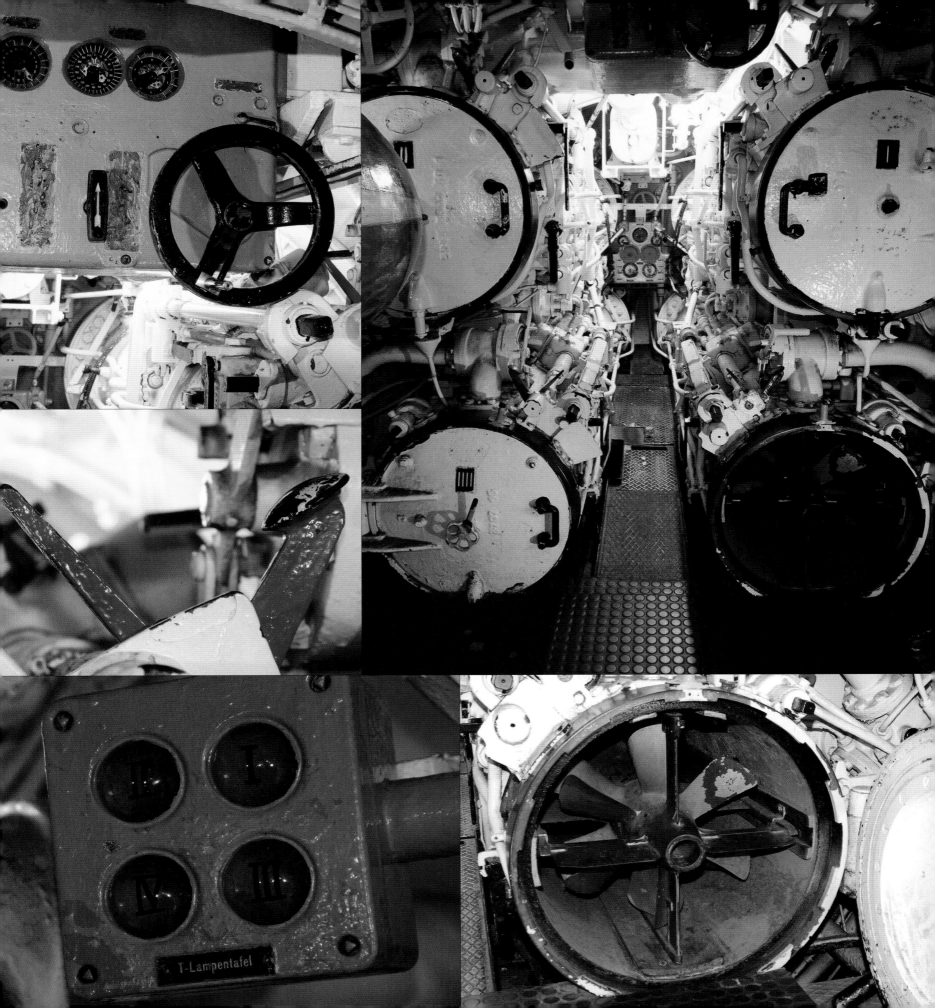

U616: First patrol (1)

The men who lived within the bow compartment represented the core of the crew—they were stationed throughout the boat, in every section. *Matrosenobergefreiter* Hans "Joe" Eckert was one of the men who went on to serve aboard *U616* in the Atlantic and Mediterranean.

"I threw in my job of repairing damaged Junkers 88 aircraft at a Volkswagen works and joined the *Kriegsmarine* intent on becoming a U-boat sailor. At the age of 18 everything was a great adventure—the six weeks' basic training to make me a seaman, marching, rifle drill, signaling, and boat work, was followed by several weeks of U-boat instruction at Pillau. Even after such a long time I can still remember marching down to the jetty with my class to go to sea in a U-boat for the first time. The U-boats were lined up in ranks like taxis, many of them the famous "canoes"—the 250-ton small boats which were really unsuitable for Atlantic work but ideal for training the thousands of sailors who were to become crews of the fast-expanding U-boat fleet. Soon after training I was en route with my kit bag to the Blohm & Voss yard at Hamburg to join the *U616*.

"My first view of the U-boat that was to play such a brief but happy and exciting time in my life was rather disappointing, as she looked like a starving horse with its steel ribs sticking out, but the classic lines of the Type VIIC U-boats were evident. I was one of the early arrivals to join the *U616* and my reception was none too warm, the commanding officer and other senior crewmembers complaining that the U-boat arm was going to the dogs, accepting pink-cheeked youngsters like me.

"Training still went on, everybody joining had to go through the boat even while it was still being built, learning every nut and bolt, where each pipe went, the color code for high-pressure air lines, low-pressure lines, and other lines that ran the length of the boats, and to be able to recognize every valve, even in the dark. The boat was commissioned on April 2, 1942, under the command of *Kptlt* Johann Spindlegger, and we were soon off to the Baltic, where training went on day and night with dozens of U-boats taking part, attacking convoys—German convoys, of course, which represented the British convoys that the U-boats would soon meet in the Atlantic. The training was very hard, and being a *Matrosenobergefreiter* with the task of loading the innumerable torpedoes fired during the exercises, with all the heaving and hauling involved, meant that I got very little sleep.

Top center: The badge of a 2nd Grade Torpedo Fire Control man, which was worn on the lower-left sleeve of the dress uniform.

Left: Greasing a torpedo before loading it into its tube. This form of regular maintenance was essential to proper torpedo performance.

Germany again. The voyage to Kristiansand was sheer hell! The weather was atrocious and the seas mountainous. In good weather the Type VIIC was a very stable craft, but in bad weather she was a pig! The boat climbed the towering waves and rushed down the other side like a demented skier. Sometimes her bows would lift to meet the next wave, sometimes she would stick her nose down and the boat would be underwater; the bridge watch, anchored to their posts by their belts clipped on to rails, would hold their breath and pray that the boat would come up again! Several boats lost all their bridge

Left: Looking forward in the bow room aboard U995, from the vantage point of the lower set of bunks on the starboard side of the U-boat.

Below: A torpedo mechanic makes fine adjustments to the internal guidance mechanisms; success or failure could depend on such minute fine-tuning.

Above: Matrosenobergefreiter Hans Eckert of U616, one of the "Ace" U-boats serving in the Mediterranean during World War II. Sixty-two boats made it past Gibraltar's defenses to the Mediterranean; U616 was the only one ever to return to the Atlantic.

"Before the training had finished, Spindlegger left the boat and went to the *U411*, only to be lost with all of his crew shortly afterward in the Mediterranean. A new commanding officer arrived—*Oblt z S* Siegfried Koitschka—a tall, powerful-looking man, a regular officer who had joined the navy in 1937. Back we went to training exercises, day and night, torpedo firing, gunnery exercises, and so forth, until the *U616* was considered efficient enough to go to the front.

"Koitschka drove us to a state of efficiency that must have been hard to match by any other boat. He had previously served as a watch officer with the famous Erich Topp, who commanded the *U552*, the 'Red Devil-boat,' so-called because of the emblem painted on the front of the conning tower. We, in turn, adopted the crest of a red devil with a pistol in each hand. Topp ended the War as the third highest-scoring U-boat captain and Koitschka brought every little last bit of his expertise to his first command.

"In February 1943 we sailed from Kiel for Norwegian waters and it would be years before most of us saw

U616: First patrol (2)

personnel in this way. And the boat itself was a shambles, smashed furniture and crockery, everything that could move, moved, and laying everywhere were groaning, vomiting sailors, praying that the nightmare would end. When on watch I was the helmsman and one of my positions was in the conning tower. Quite often I would be up to my neck in the North Sea as the freezing water poured through the upper hatch. Steering the boat was almost impossible and I just hung on for grim life, spewing my heart up. Koitschka and a few members of the crew who were not seasick brought the boat into harbor.

"On April 10, *U616* left Norway for her first patrol into the Atlantic, where the life of a U-boat could be measured in days. Again, the weather was bad and all I remember of this first patrol was the bad weather, being bombed by aircraft, attacking a destroyer, and a continuous flow of signals and decoding in the wardroom, a sure sign that great events were taking place just over the horizon! In recent years I found out that we had been taking part in the biggest convoy battle of the War against convoys HX229 and SC122 in March 1943, the month in which the fortunes of the U-boats started to steadily decline.

"[After this mission] we returned to the French port of St Nazaire, parked the boat in a bunker and went ashore for a glorious few weeks.

Below left: Thick plumes of smoke signal the end of a tanker—prime targets among Allied convoy traffic. The stern of the departing U-boat is just visible (bottom left).
Below right: Allied air power would prove to be a key factor in the defeat of Dönitz's U-boat service, particularly once radar had been mounted in Allied bombers.

When we sailed again we had been at sea for a few days before Koitschka announced that we were going into the Mediterranean. Our hearts sank because no U-boat had ever entered and returned from the Mediterranean, and getting past Gibraltar—probably the hottest place in the world for any passing U-boat—was nearly impossible. But Koitschka was by now admired by the crew for his ability, toughness, and great sense of humor, and he took the *U616* through on the surface at night and with no trouble from the Tommies, who must have been asleep. We operated off Oran and attacked a destroyer without success, although we heard the torpedoes detonate. On May 13 we left the area to proceed to our base: La Spezia in Italy. But British aircraft attacked us. We dived in a shower of bombs but thought nothing more of it until our 'listener' reported the sound of propellers of fast-moving warships several hours later, and we went deep to avoid any unpleasantness. We were soon down to 500ft [152m], moving at slow speed and keeping as quiet as a mouse, but our 'listener' soon dampened our hopes of creeping away by announcing an enemy coming in to attack. At the right moment we sped

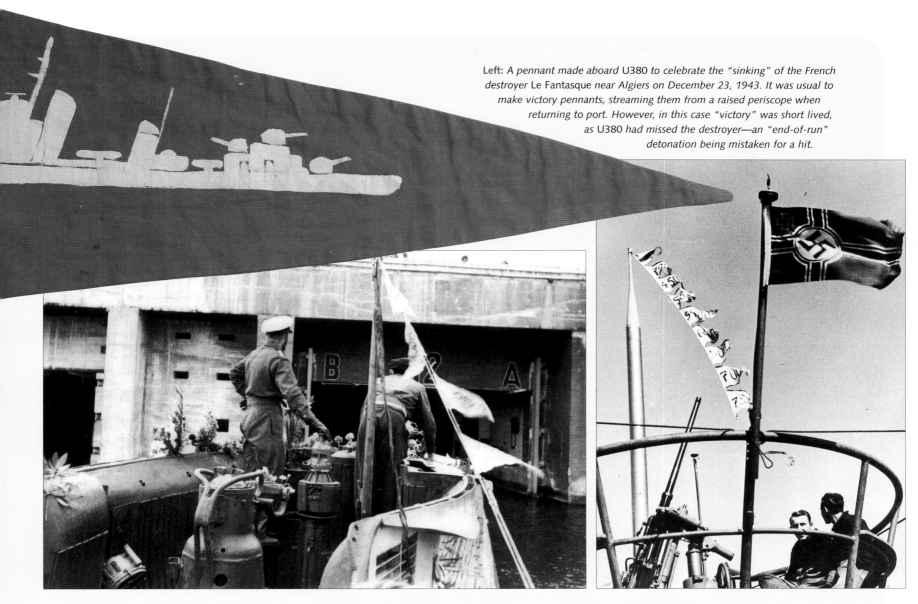

Left: *A pennant made aboard U380 to celebrate the "sinking" of the French destroyer* Le Fantasque *near Algiers on December 23, 1943. It was usual to make victory pennants, streaming them from a raised periscope when returning to port. However, in this case "victory" was short lived, as U380 had missed the destroyer—an "end-of-run" detonation being mistaken for a hit.*

up and went hard-a-port but the first pattern of depth charges came down on top of us with an ear-shattering, thunderous crash. Our faithful U-boat staggered and creaked and threatened to implode but she slowly regained her poise. Down came more depth charges but one ship in the group above us seemed more persistent than the others and dropped her charges on target every time. The boat was a mess, with gauges smashed, air lines ruptured, the main compass in pieces, and water spraying into the boat—and still the charges came down relentlessly. The diesel engines were damaged, as were the electric motors, several cells of the battery were cracked, and the radio was out of order. A charge that exploded quite close to the bows threatened to stave the hull of the boat in. After three hours we were thinking that we would have to go up and scuttle the boats when suddenly our tormentors went away. After the War I discovered that our attackers had been HMS *Haydon*, USS *Kalk*, HMS *Calpe*, and USS *Strive*. Our main tormentor turned out to be HMS *Haydon*, whose captain wanted to stay and sink us but he was outranked by the captain of USS *Kalk* so he had to follow his orders and sail for Gibraltar. On arrival at La Spezia it was found that our torpedo tubes had been slewed sideways by the depth charges and these had to be replaced. The nightmare of that attack stayed with me long after the War had ended."

Above left: *Erich Topp (in white cap) brings his famous "Red Devil" boat U552 into St Nazaire's U-boat bunker, his patrol's success spelled out in victory pennants.*

Above right: *The accuracy of tonnage claims made by U-boat commanders varied wildly, especially after underwater attacks became the norm, which meant that results could not always be verified.*

Harsh conditions

Conditions in the forward torpedo room were difficult in the extreme for the numerous crewmen who had to live and work in the confined space. After the War, Klaus Andersen, captain of *U481*, described what the enlisted men, in particular, had endured during combat patrol:

"People have an uncanny ability to endure harsh conditions, no matter how difficult they may be, and even consider such adverse conditions 'normal.' I always had great problems with the foul air. Even with ventilation fans running efficiently there were parts of the boat where the putrid air hardly stirred. I got over this problem by spending most of my time in the central control room or in the tower, where there was usually a good supply of fresh air, but the poor men in the bow torpedo room—or even worse, in the oily atmosphere of the engine room—must have suffered enormously.

"Although I served in U-boats, the question I still cannot answer for myself is how the 'Lords' actually lived in the bow torpedo room. They were squashed together worse than sardines and yet they survived without an eruption of uncontrolled aggression. In fact, I cannot remember ever having to deal with disciplinary matters arising from those exceptionally cramped quarters. The senior men there who kept those harsh quarters running smoothly were never really appreciated for their sterling performance."

Despite the difference in size between Germany's U-boat types, life for ordinary seamen within the forward torpedo room followed a common pattern. Wolfgang Schiller was aboard the Type IXC *U505*.

"Of course, the torpedo room was very narrow. You can't think of it as it is today on display in the US [in the Museum of Science, Chicago, IL] where it is just practically an empty room. There, where we're standing nowadays, was a torpedo! On the torpedo was our table—you could see where we ate. We sat with our bottoms on the bunk and ate on this wooden plank that sat on the torpedo. As for the sleeping situation, I can say the following: the individual people who went on watch had rotation bunks. The bunks were never cold, they were always warm. One got out, and the next got in, because every four hours they had to be rotated. The people had to go on watch, and there were a limited number of bunks. The first people aboard the sub were lying

Above: A torpedo being loaded into Tube 1 aboard a Type VII U-boat. This arduous task required bunks to be stowed to provide space, and so off-duty crew (such as the man still reading his newspaper in this photo) had to find space wherever they could, in order to allow the torpedo crew to go about their work.

Left: Looking sternward from the torpedo tubes aboard U995. The near left-hand bunks have been removed, and a strip light added for visitors. The compartment appears spacious—until one considers the number of men living and working in this space.

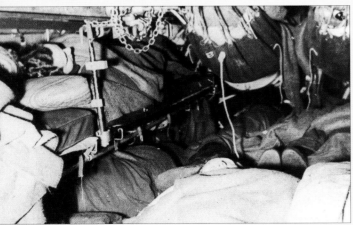

somehow on a sack or in a hammock—for example, the *Smutje* [cook] hung here mostly in the middle over the torpedo because he didn't have a bunk either. They were the so-called 'free watchmen,' and these 'free-runners' got no bunk. Although I got a special bunk, this bunk wasn't taken enthusiastically by anyone, because you couldn't relax in it. You had to lie only on your back; you

couldn't turn over because of this thick pipe up above your head. And naturally, that was a situation, too, that you could only lay on your back for a little while, mostly. And during rough seas, I always steadied myself on [the pipe] with my knee. And one day, during really rough seas, I flew right out—along with the whole bunk—out of the mountings and fell onto the back of the next guy.

"Our free time can be expressed as follows: I'm a book-worm, still am today. Today I read English books, too. Back then, I also made the effort to read as much as I could. I had a great deal of success making myself comfortable in that fashion to keep my nerves. And if we were able to have a card game, and that wasn't possible at all because of the watch shifts, we would have been pretty lucky.

"To add something about music or entertainment—back then we had a record player on board, and the record player could play German records and songs for us. So we listened to a little music. I can't recall anymore whether we could receive radio music over the antenna. If so, at best American or Spanish, right in that area where we were.

"As far as our own music went, I can only remember 'Lili Marlene' and such things—light music was perhaps predominant. I hardly think that as young people we had much interest in operas and operettas, if you want to say it like that—an expression in German like *'am Hut haben'* ['have it on the hat']. So we probably had more light music. Back then the pop songs were already getting big—it was 1942—we had the chance once in a while to hear American or English records. Maybe you can remember 'Lili Marlene' and such things. That was naturally a little soothing for the nerves for us, you could say.

"As far as I can remember, we naturally had our 'homework' to do. In terms of 'refreshing our knowledge,' what we had learned at torpedo school. We knew to master our tasks practically on the submarine, in life. For the sub, it was important for each individual not only to fill his own position, but also others: to be able to help in case of difficulty. Everyone filled in for everyone else; it was a necessity. Also, if, for example, during whatever engagement someone went down, others had to be able to take over. So, we were very well-rounded in that respect, and that interested us as well, and we got the material right in our hand, so that we could act in the respective manner."

Below: *Preparing food on the small, detachable drop-leaf tables within the bow room. Hammocks increased the number of bunk spaces available.*

Left: *With a full load of torpedoes, provisions, and crew in the bow room, space was scarce, as this photo shows. The desire to see some action was no doubt enhanced by the knowledge that, for every torpedo fired, a little more living space became available, as the stored-up ammunition was used.*

Torpedoes and the Torpedo Crisis

"I refused to burden U-boats with these wretched things any longer."—Karl Dönitz

Somewhat surprisingly, given their reputation for ruthless efficiency, the U-boat service's torpedoes were remarkably unreliable throughout World War II. This was due to a combination of problems that were not fully solved until 1942—and then almost by accident. (Arguably it was not fully understood until after the War.) The root cause of this malfunctioning weaponry was the negligible development that had taken place in German torpedo design between World Wars I and II.

Above: *Karl Dönitz (center) and BdU staff officers on the balcony of their Kernevel headquarters, near Lorient. Dönitz knew that many of the torpedoes supplied to the U-boats malfunctioned, and he had to handle the crews' resulting frustration deftly.*

There were two basic types of U-boat torpedo: those that were driven by an internal combustion engine which was fed with fuel, steam, and compressed air, designated the G7a and known as the *"Ato,"* and those propelled by an electric motor: the G7e, or *"Eto."* The primary advantage of the *"Ato"* was its longer range, although it betrayed its position by emitting a stream of bubbles in its wake. The *"Eto"* did not do this, and was also ultimately cheaper to produce.

The Torpedo Experimental Institute had found during test firings in 1936 that both weapons had a tendency to run deeper than set. Although a counter-measure "depth spring" was designed, the Institute placed so much faith in their newly developed magnetic warhead—which was triggered by running *beneath* a ship's magnetic field rather than using a contact fuse—that the deep-running problem was not at the time considered noteworthy.

During 1940 and the invasion of Norway, these magnetic fuses were discovered to be faulty—it was thought that they were badly affected by the earth's magnetic field at northern latitudes. Suddenly, the deep-running issue was recognized to be a very real problem. As the new four-pronged trigggers also had a tendency to malfunction (they had been tested with only two trial shots in 1937), the torpedoes were effectively found to be useless. So much so that several U-boats forming a protective screen at the mouth of Narvik's entrance fjord were presented with numerous opportunities to attack British warships intent on disrupting German landings—only to be thwarted by their own torpedoes. The British forces concerned went on to sink ten German destroyers and other ancillary shipping before sailing from the confined waterways untroubled by the U-boats. No less a commander than Günther Prien, of *U47* and Scapa Flow fame, attempted to attack Allied vessels unloading troops in Vaags Fjord. Four torpedoes were fired, but all missed. Miraculously, despite then running aground, *U47* remained undetected and Prien was able to free the boat and retreat. Despite the strong U-boat force deployed during the Norwegian invasion, no successes were achieved along the coast, while six U-boats were lost. Morale slumped so badly that Dönitz's Chief of Operations, Eberhard Godt, stated that he could no longer take any responsibility for sending his men into action with such blunt weapons.

Ironically it was by copying British contact pistols, captured from HMS *Seal* on May 5, 1940, that the Germans' trigger difficulties were solved. But not until January 1942 did the crew of *U94* identify the source of the deep-running problem. It transpired that the torpedoes' balance chambers (these housed the hydrostatic valves that controlled the weapon's depth) were faulty, and leaked badly. The fault was in turn caused by the increase in air pressure that occurred when a U-boat was submerged, or launching a weapon. The pressure was being transferred into the balance chamber, altering the settings and sending the torpedoes deep. By February 1942, steps had been taken to rectify the fault, and the *Kriegsmarine* was finally able to fight with a more reliable weapon.

Above: *Using the specially designed cradle, a torpedo is lowered through the bow compartment's loading hatch on a Type VIIC U-boat.*

Left: *Günther Prien's fury at attacks being thwarted by faulty torpedoes removed any doubts about the U-boats' weaponry. Prien (left), a forthright, daring commander, remained one of the U-bootwaffe's leading lights until his death in 1941.*

Right: *The breeches of bow Tubes 1 and 3 on U995. The open Tube 3 carries a G7e electric torpedo.*

Moldy bread—and "eels"

Alongside Wolfgang Schiller aboard *U505* was Hans Goebeler, an electrician's mate assigned to work on the boat's electric motors.

"When I joined the *Kriegsmarine*, I was 17 years old and at 18 I became a crewmember of *U505*. After performing a quarter of a year's basic training in a big naval training center in Bourg Leopold, Belgium (learning how to creep across sand dunes!), I spent another quarter of a year in U-boat school studying electrical engineering at the 1st ULD (*U-Boot-Lehr* Division) at Pillau, East Prussia, on the Baltic. Because of my good review, I was ordered directly to the 2nd U-boat Flotilla at Lorient, on the French Atlantic coast, instead of a shipyard in Germany, where submarines were built.

"More than 95 per cent of all submarine crews who had volunteered for the Navy were hand-picked out of thousands after they went through different physical and psychological examinations. At that time, belonging to the Submarine Forces had been a distinction, and our spirits were high—we had a strong belief to fight for our country. Until the end of the War the Submarine Service had never been short of volunteers. We had a very rough and hard drill, but we knew that without it there was only little chance to survive . . . we had to know every handle, valve, cranny, and nook, even in darkness . . . but also a lot of theory.

"The torpedo tubes were loaded with 'Aale' [eels]. In other navies they called them 'fish' but we called them 'eels.' Front and aft torpedo rooms were sleeping and living rooms at the same time for off-watch crew too, but there were also up to six torpedoes stored and tied down in the front room, which had to be used as sleeping places for four poor sailors, who slept on top of them. In the aft torpedo room there were three torpedoes tied down—these also were used as sleeping places for two off-watch sailors—and four or six hours later [they were again] used by those who had been on watch during that time. But very often they could not use their greasy beds because the torpedo mechanics had to maintain the *Aale*. It was the same thing in using the bunks. These were still warm when the guy who came in from watch tried to find a couple of hours' sleep. Anyhow, more torpedoes were stored outside the pressure hull on the so-called 'free-flooding' upper deck in pressure and waterproof tubes. It always had been a most dangerous business getting them from the upper deck either into the front or back torpedo rooms at sea because until this hard job was done, there was no chance of diving. With the torpedo hatch open the boat would sink within a couple of minutes' time.

"Now let's carry on getting the boat loaded with only necessary things: the seabags stacked high between the torpedo tubes were left there till all those boxes, crates, cartons, cans, and a lot more little and big things were stored in [their] places by storing list and number behind the electric engines, the diesels, even some things in the bilges. Sacks of potatoes were squeezed beside the chart table in the control room, where they started to rot, right after the first time we submerged. Can you imagine the stinking smell, mixed with the scent of diesel fuel and everything that produces a perfume or odor more or less of its own nature, even the bodies of 60 men?

"Hammocks and nets filled with fresh bread, which became moldy after just two or three days, were strung up high in the torpedo hatch area front and back. Even when there were only little pieces left—which were kind of white-looking instead of green—we ate them. All this made the U-boat look more like a bazaar than a weapon of war. But each time we had to repeat this maneuver, we became less bothered by it all. At this phase of the War, our U-boats were still on the winning side and having great luck on the hunt so there wasn't anything that could change our minds."

Above left: *Hoisting a torpedo ready for loading. Behind* Matrosengefreiter *Herman Hausruckinger (foreground) can be seen a white pith helmet—this U-boat, U564, was Caribbean-bound.*

Below right: *The girder from which torpedoes—even mines—were hung for loading and unloading from the tubes. The rear pulley moved it sideways, while the near one raised or lowered it.*

Below and right: An off-duty crewman on U564 reads in his bunk while others reload the tubes. Mechanikerobergefreiter Wilhelm Bigge attaches the girder to a torpedo on the floor—the first of the reloads.

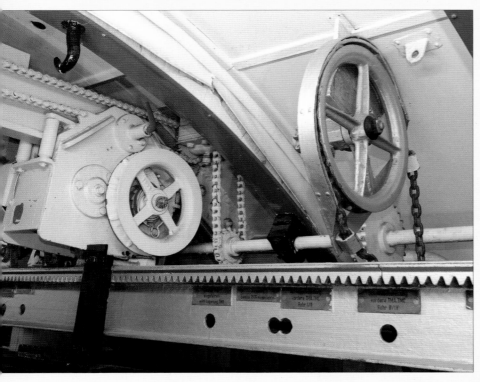

Suhren remembers

The forward torpedo room was a particularly difficult place to live in at the beginning of a patrol, when the small compartment was used for the storage of food as well as weaponry. Reinhard "Teddy" Suhren, commander of U564, remembered:

"During my operations [as captain] I was always aboard a Type VIIC U-boat of about 750 tons and a highest possible speed of 15 to 16 knots surfaced, 7 to 8 knots submerged. The crew consisted of about 46 men. The life for the crew in the bow room of the ship was very hard because when we left port we had four torpedoes above the bilge, so that altogether in that compartment we had ten torpedoes. The two above the bilge were covered with sheets of wood and on those the men had to eat. Also, the bunks were here, too. Right above them was scaffolding on which the torpedoes had to be hoisted for loading and unloading the tubes, meaning that the men had hardly any room to move about, and if they did, they had to be on all fours. Even if the sea was reasonably calm, you always had the odd wave rocking the ship—and the pea soup ended up everywhere!"

Below: Mealtime in the bow compartment of U564; pea soup is consumed while sitting on piles of food and munitions.

Lucky strikes

An array of warhead fuses and steering devices could be fitted to the basic torpedo bodies of the two stock types used in World War II. The fuses themselves proved problematic and, as Reimar Ziesmar of *U38* remembered, at least one ship was sunk without being hit by an active warhead at all:

"Eight merchant ships fell victim to *U38*, but only in connection with two ships have some unusual events become etched in my mind. The first ship sunk on that patrol was SS *Japan* and it sticks in my head because I directed the gunfire that sank her, one of my duties as IIWO. The next was our eighth ship sunk—the British SS *Kingston Hill*—on June 6, 1941, during our homebound journey, bringing the tonnage to 200,000 tons on the account of *Kptlt* Liebe and thus qualifying him for decoration. But it was a rather peculiar attack: I had the watch in the conning tower in a really dark, black night. By chance I saw in the narrow sector of my binoculars a faint, reddish, slightly wavering light. After waking *Kptlt* Liebe and urging him to go after it, a large shadow popped up in the darkness. *U38* slowed down to avoid the glimmer of our wake produced by micro-organisms in the warm sea water. But what to do? *U38* had only two torpedoes, both with uncertain functional value. One

had no ignition pistol in its explosive head—it was damaged during reloading from the German supply ship *Egerland* that we had met with in the South Atlantic—and the other torpedo showed some irregularities in its steering apparatus. Thirdly, after the gun attack on SS *Japan*, there were no shells left.

"After some quick arguments, *Kptlt* Liebe decided to release the second torpedo with the bad steerage. But after firing, it developed a circular pattern and followed a course headed back at *U38*! We were forced to go after it at full speed until its running capacity was exhausted. By doing this *U38* stirred up an enormously phosphorescent swell that alerted the [British] ship's crew. We saw electric torches speeding aft where we supposed their deck gun was located. *U38* stopped abruptly, thereafter slowly drawing back so that the men at the gun could see nothing, and they didn't release a single shot. Because my 20mm Flak gun was too short-range, and in any event had no use against such large game, I urged *Kptlt* Liebe to try the torpedo without the ignition pistol, thinking that at least it would make a hole in the hull of the vessel, and if correctly placed, it could stop the ship and eventually flood it. And so it happened. The torpedo crew fired our last 'eel'—which struck. The ship stopped and one, or one and a half hours after the impact the ship began to sink, the crew going without haste into their lifeboats undisturbed by us. Arriving back in Lorient, *U38* had no ammunition and only one ton of diesel oil left."

Above and top center: Stamped on the reverse with a serial number and Kriegsmarine insignia, this stopwatch was owned by Obermaschinist Ernst Pöhlitz of U929. The timepiece was standard issue.

With the failure of the early torpedoes, the most effective weapon in the U-boat's arsenal was the magnetic mine. Jürgen Oesten laid a field of mines near Newcastle, England, during 1940 with his Type IIC *U61*.

"I was actually ordered to mine the Firth of Forth, but couldn't get in. A friend of mine in *U21*, Frauenheim, had been there already and damaged

Left: A very rare photograph of an engineering officer on the stern wintergarten aboard a Type VIID minelayer; the vertical mine chutes are visible on the stern deck. Only seven of these boats were built, and five of them were lost in action.

Left: *Success! Its back broken, an armed merchant ship sinks, watched by its attackers. Magnetically triggered torpedoes were designed to achieve this type of structural damage, exploding beneath their target—the shock wave breaking the hull in two.*

Right: *A late-War Type VIIC approaches merchant shipping. The small aerial on the bridge is for the "Naxos" radar detector, first issued to combat boats in September 1943.*

the cruiser HMS *Belfast* in November 1939. He had dropped his mines inside the Firth of Forth. The cruiser was at anchor and when it swung around it went over one of the mines and was severely damaged. I dropped mines at Tynemouth at the entrance of the river Tyne leading to Newcastle. I laid a field directly in front of this entrance. I had been ordered to go into the Firth of Forth during the previous mission but the chances were very slim. The British had very heavy defenses, including defensive mines. It was a very small entrance guarded on both sides and any ships going in and out had to pass through there.

So that, I thought, was just too much of a risk to take and so I took the mines back to Wilhelmshaven. You see, it was within the control of the commander at sea to judge his situation and you want at least a 30 per cent chance of survival. So, upon my return I said that the mission did not have enough chance and Dönitz took it for granted that I was right and had no objections.

"With the magnetic mines you could put a maximum of three in each torpedo tube. These small boats had only three bow torpedo tubes, each of which could hold either two TMC or three TMB mines—Torpedo Mine Type B and C."

Above: *Binoculars used by Oblt z S Harald Lange aboard U505, the only U-boat to be captured intact by the US Navy, on June 4, 1944. Folding eyepieces allowed special shaded goggles to be worn.*

Left: *The bow room of a Type II U-boat was especially crowded. The entire crew lived in this tiny compartment, with little differentiation between officers and enlisted men.*

Warrant and Commissioned Officers' Quarters

"Officers and men lived so close together . . . they shared the same fate, so everyone felt equally important."—Reinhard Suhren, *U564*

Left: *Looking sternward on* U995 *from the warrant officers' sleeping and messing quarters. The circular hatchway in the background leads into the control room.*

Through a narrow doorway immediately astern of the bow compartment was the forward head, located to port; a small provisions locker was to starboard. Abaft of this was the small compartment that served as the warrant officers' quarters (*Oberfeldwebelraum*). Here, the senior non-commissioned officers used the four bunks available (two bunks were situated on either side of the main walkway). Unlike in the bow compartment, no one here was obliged to share his precious bed. The men who typically resided here were the heads of the diesel engine and electric motor sections. Each of the boat's two propulsion methods came directly within the broad remit of the chief engineer. However, an *Obermaschinist* dedicated to his particular section—diesel engines or electric motors—handled the smooth running of the machinery. With large amounts of time aboard U-boats spent surfaced, either in transit or during convoy attacks, the man responsible for the electric motors could also double as cover for the starboard diesel, leaving another to watch the port engine.

The *Obersteuermann*, the boat's navigator, was also responsible for the Third Watch while the boat was traveling on the surface. Additionally, he doubled as quartermaster aboard the boat, and would oversee provisioning and the even distribution of the stored food before leaving port.

The crew chief aboard a Type VIIC, the *Bootsmann*, was commonly referred to by the men as "Number One." His primary role—assisted by a pair of bosun's mates (*Bootsmannsmaate*)—was to maintain discipline among the enlisted men. He was also the first port of call if there were any problems within the crew, unless these became sufficiently serious to warrant being dealt with by an officer. The *Bootsmann* held enough authority to deal with minor problems himself. He also took care of the upkeep of the men's clothing and equipment, and was responsible for general order and cleanliness aboard the boat. The *Bootsmann* was also attached to one of the rotating watches atop the conning tower.

During any kind of torpedo action the *Bootsmann*'s station was within the cramped conning tower, manning the torpedo calculator into which he would program information relayed from either the captain at the periscope or the IWO (First Watch Officer) at the surface-targeting device on the bridge (this consisted of binoculars mounted on a pedestal sight). The information inputted would be transmitted direct to the torpedo room. When attacking with the deck gun, the *Bootsmann* led the artillery crew.

Immediately adjacent to the warrant officers' quarters was the officers' room (*Offiziersraum*), which was occupied by the boat's commissioned officers. Here, the First and Second Watch Officers (IWO and IIWO) and the Chief Engineer (*Leitender Ingenieur*, or "LI") slept. At this part of the boat the pressure hull reached its widest as it tapered away to both bow and stern. Thus the bunks for the officers were recessed further from the central passageway and there was also room for four small closets in which the officers stored whatever personal possessions they took to sea. To port, a small drop-leaf table was fitted, which allowed the compartment to double as a wardroom, where all the officers, captain included, would eat their meals in relative comfort. It was behind this table that the chief engineer would sleep, generally on the green leather bench seat although a folding bunk was also available.

The IWO was the boat's executive officer, second-in-command to the captain. He was responsible for the First Watch and also for the maintenance of the torpedoes and their fire-control systems, in which duties the *Mechanikersmaat* (stationed within the bow compartment) assisted him closely. During surfaced torpedo attacks, the IWO would actually aim and fire the torpedoes from the bridge, allowing the captain to maintain an all-round perspective.

The IIWO was the boat's junior officer. He headed the Second Watch on the bridge and also oversaw the maintenance of the boat's artillery, both deck gun and Flak weaponry. Combined with many smaller administrative tasks, the IIWO would also occasionally decode any classified radio traffic transmitted by BdU to the boat at sea.

The remaining members of the crew—the petty officers—were stationed astern, past the control room in their own quarters, the *Unteroffiziersraum*. Here, the 11 petty officers that manned a Type VIIC shared eight bunks in rotation, while two drop-leaf tables similar to those found forward allowed a rudimentary messing arrangement. Here, the bosun's mates, two senior radio crewmen (*Funkmaate*), and middle-ranking engineers for both the diesel engines and the electric motors (*Maschinenmaate*) lived while at sea, their personal belongings again squeezed into the small number of lockers lining the interior of the pressure hull.

None of these quarters doubled as any kind of action station; they were inhabited strictly by men who were off-watch. It was not uncommon for a combat boat to be accompanied on patrol by extra crew in the form of propaganda reporters (such as in the critically acclaimed film *Das Boot*), or officers in training. These men, too, would be distributed between the three compartments, as were the medical officers, who would occasionally go to sea on combat missions, though more often aboard the larger Type IX U-boats than the Type VIIC.

Page right, clockwise from top left: Petty officers enjoy a drink aboard U608 (the compartment's top bunks have been folded up and out of the way to give extra headroom); the petty officers' compartment aboard U995, showing the same bunks in their normal position (seen through the open hatchway is the well of the attack periscope dominating the aft portion of the control room); petty officer's service jacket—the rank is denoted by the metal collar flashes; the officers' mess aboard U995, the small table offset to port.

Kronenberg's cap

Service cap of the chief engineer aboard *U453*, a Type VIIC transferred to the Mediterranean in November 1941. *Oblt (Ing)* Werner Kronenberg joined *U453* in August 1942, sailing on ten combat missions. Later posted to the training boat *U555*, he was awarded the German Cross in Gold on March 29, 1944.

The "notches" Kronenberg made on his cap's chin strap denoted ships claimed sunk by torpedo, minelaying missions (three) and their claimed victims (four!), and aircraft shot down (two).

U-boat crews commonly decorated both their boat and their headgear with unofficial symbols—in this instance, a felt Mickey Mouse.

Supply run to Norway

Obermaschinenmaat Herbert Wien served aboard the oddity that was *UA*—a large boat constructed for the Turkish navy as the *Batiray* but which was commissioned into the *Kriegsmarine* on September 20, 1939, as the outbreak of war prevented its delivery. Large and unwieldy, the boat's first mission was a supply run to Norway.

"Our new crew comprised 41 men, four officers, and a Medical Officer, Dr Helmut Richter. I had already served two years in the *Kriegsmarine*, as *Obermaschinenmaat* on the two training boats *U2* and *U7* sailing out of Neustadt. We were a good crew that gathered at *UA* in September 1939 to take the boat out to sea. However, it was hard work for us machinists, as all of the boat's instructions needed translation from Turkish to German! So we began working on labeling important switches and valves, and committing them all to memory. But after weeks and days had passed we were glad when we had finished and could leave the Germaniawerft at the end of November. With our boat we had a nice secure mooring space on the Tirpitz Mole in Kiel's naval base, near our depot ship, *Usambara*.

Above: Grade three electrician trade badge, worn on lower left sleeve of dress uniform.

"Testing the boat began immediately at the beginning of December under the upper supervision of *K z S* Bräutigam. Several submerged operations, alarm diving into the Kiel Bay as well as adjusting the gyroscope compass installation, took us through the rest of 1939. Then it was a vacation for all, through Christmas to the New Year. There was more testing after New Year, in the deep water of Danzig Bay in the Baltic. With the deep-diving tests we exceeded our shipyard-rated depth for our riveted boat without problems. For us this was a calming bit of knowledge. At the beginning of February there was another short stay in the shipyard for overhaul and some rust repairs.

"The beginning of March found us practicing day and night shooting in Flensburger Förde. In fact, it was not only for the torpedo men but also for the seamen personnel, and especially for us on the electric motors. Our chief engineer was anxious to make us totally familiar with all eventualities that we could expect to encounter in the future. At that time the experiences of boats from the front line to the 'Wegener' flotilla were already common knowledge, so we had an idea of what to expect.

"The first mission finally arrived. On April 9, 1940, the occupation of Denmark began, as did the invasion of Norway. Events seemed to rush toward us now. The fact that we were headed for Norway soon got around. We were, at this time, the largest boat in the U-boat service, which also included our fuel bunker capacity. So, in order to make the most of this, we were selected to supply *Luftwaffe* units in Norway with aviation fuel. We took onboard only the absolutely necessary amount of diesel to allow the storage of aviation fuel in the majority of our fuel bunkers. In order to use our cells for this, the filling and emptying mechanisms had to be converted, which was soon done.

"So, eventually we were scheduled to carry:
165 cu m [216 cu yd] of aviation fuel;
5 cu m [6½ cu yd] of oil for the *Luftwaffe* engines;
90 cu m [118 cu yd] of oil for U-boats;
One entire dissembled 88mm Flak cannon and
1,150 rounds of ammunition;
15,250kg [33,620lb] *Luftwaffe* bombs.

"All in all, it was a highly explosive freight, which meant it was absolutely forbidden to smoke anywhere on the entire boat—including the conning tower and upper deck. With more than a few mixed feelings we left Kiel in the middle of April. We stopped briefly

Above: Loading supplies aboard a Type VIIC. Everything had to be passed through one of four small hatchways, or be dismantled to fit.

Above: *A petty officer at the port engine telegraph aboard UA. The crewman's U-boat is clearly identifiable by his cap badge, which features a Sperm Whale.*

in Heligoland, where we removed our bow's wooden ice protection, staying there overnight. The next morning there was a low-hanging cloud cover with a fresh seasonal breeze. We departed the German Bight undisturbed and steered toward the Norwegian coast. That morning as the weather worsened we practiced a crash dive. I heard someone on the bridge say, 'wind force 7,' and the swell picked up accordingly. The further we traveled, the worse the weather became. Our goal was Trondheim. No one knew how far the English naval forces were from our position. After approximately five days we were off the entrance to the fjord. While submerged, our commander marked out possible navigation aids and after two days we were ready to enter the fjord under a black night sky. Aboard the boat the situation was uncertain and loaded with tension. A hardly visible shadow became a small patrol ship. Then suddenly from the darkness comes a call with the 'Whisper Bag' [megaphone]: 'Is *Obersteuermann* Arnaschuss on board?' The answer 'Yes' quickly flies back from our bridge. The small ship *Kolcher* guides us to our mooring place. It turned out that the patrol ship's *Obersteuermann* and ours were old comrades. We were all glad, the first round was completed!

"Over the next few days we finished our mission with the unloading of our cargo. The aviation fuel was unloaded into a small lighter. With empty bunkers we dived several times into a deep part of the fjord to flush out the remainder of the gasoline and our task was over. Despite the fighting in Norway our return trip to Kiel passed without incident.

Above: *A Maschinenmaat* shows some trainee engineers behind him (out of shot) how to use the electric motor.
Left: *A gift for his wife made by U377's Obermaschinist Jak Mallmann in Spitzbergen, Norway, on November 4, 1942.*

Still, another short stay in the Germaniawerft was necessary in order to redo the filling and flushing fuel mechanisms back to 'normal.' Nonetheless, an explosion in one of the fuel bunkers scared the hell out of us. A shipyard worker was badly injured nearby. The cause? Sparks from a defective cable lamp igniting fuel vapor!"

Extraordinary missions

Aboard *U57* (a Type IIC U-boat) there were no separate quarters for non-commissioned officers. In 1940, the crew were curious about the sudden arrival of a new petty officer—his role aboard ship being deliberately kept vague until it was time for him to fulfil his assigned task. The captain, Erich Topp, described the task of landing a saboteur on the English coast:

Above: *Erich Topp on his bridge. Topp became the third most successful U-boat commander in terms of tonnage sunk.*

"Although I never was equipped with mines—I only had torpedoes on board—the only thing I once had to do before the [sinking of *U57* in the] Elbe was to bring ashore a sabotage troop. Not a troop, but one man. That was in the Thames estuary; I dropped a man there. When he said goodbye to me, well, I wished him good luck for his operations and he said, 'I am very familiar with England—I have been living there for many, many years, so it's no problem to me. You have treated me on board very well. I want to thank you, so what can I bring you with me when I come back?' So I said, 'Bring yourself!'

"Because, I said, from my point of view it was a very dangerous task he had there. But he said, 'No, no, what can I bring you with me?' Well, at that time the most fascinating thing was a Dunhill pipe. I was smoking pipes at the time, I even had on board on my little turret, the bridge, I had a special box fitted for my pipe that I could close when I was diving.

"Anyhow, I heard nothing of him. After one year, or perhaps one and a quarter, we were sitting in St Nazaire in the mess and talking, talking, talking, and somebody, a man, came in and sat beside us at another table as was the norm. I did not recognize his face at all, or notice him really. Minutes later, the man stood up and approached me. He said, 'Herr Topp, I have something for you,' and produced a Dunhill pipe. Indeed it was the same man, although he had changed and was now with a beard. He had made no sabotage but had collected much information, though I had never expected to see him again, nor did I ever expect to receive the pipe that he had promised so long ago. Unfortunately it was stolen, you know, in Gotenhafen. It was stolen with some other things of mine later in the War."

In May 1943 Dönitz ordered that seven U-boats were to be converted into "Flak traps" (*Flakfallen*), which involved adding heavy anti-aircraft weaponry. The task of the "Flak traps" was to accompany outgoing U-boats, and to counter any aerial threat with a strong barrage of Flak. The boats carried an additional man—a doctor—in recognition of the casualties likely to result from this dangerous task. Aboard *U441*, *Kptlt* Götz von Hartmann had taken Paul Pfaffinger onto his crew roster.

"I had been in command of *U563* as part of the 1st U-Flotilla in Brest. However, the boat had received damage and needed to be returned to the Blohm & Voss yards in Germany, so I handed it over to Klaus Bargsten. My full crew and I transferred to a new boat. My chief engineer was, thank God, very experienced as he had been a *Standartenführer* in the naval SA before the War, and had also been a *Maschinenmaat* on Hersing's boat during World War I!

"So, in April 1943 I took command of *U441*, a Type VIIC which was converting to a 'Flak trap.' The captain had, confusingly, been Klaus

Below: *The stern* Wintergarten *aboard U995, carrying the 37mm heavy Flak cannon, added later in the War as a defense against larger enemy aircraft including bombers. The resulting overall increase in weight proved problematic, though, and moves to reduce and redistribute it included the removal of the forward deck cannon.*

Left: *The conning tower of U995 looking sternward. In the foreground is the main hatch and raised attack periscope. Behind is the upper Wintergarten, with its twin-barreled 20mm Flak weapons; a ready-use pressure-tight ammunition container is just visible behind the periscope housing.*

Right: *This pre-War Type II U-boat with its tiny bridge is notable for its lack of anti-aircraft weaponry. Six of these boats would later be given extended Wintergartens after transferring to the Black Sea to engage with the Russians.*

Below: *One extreme in air defense—U441, one of Dönitz's seven "Flak trap" U-boats. Ultimately, the experiment failed, with U-boats proving to be very unsteady as gun platforms.*

Hartmann. Within the flotilla we were nicknamed: I was 'Hartmann blue' and he was 'Hartmann brown'—not because he was in any way related to the Nazis (the so-called 'brown party'), but because of our different eye color! He had become very ill, so we took command of his boat. However, we weren't overly happy about the whole idea of the Flak trap, and within earshot of my men they were being labeled as taking part in a suicide mission and became slightly despondent.

"Luckily, unlike our last boat, because of the special nature of our mission we also took a doctor aboard. He was quartered in the *Oberfeldwebelraum* and again, as luck would have it, he was a very competent seaman. He had already earned the Iron Cross First Class at sea, and was a keen sportsman as well. On our first mission sure enough we attracted the enemy's attention. Three Beaufighters attacked us and although our gunners put up some fierce Flak we were left with 13 wounded and ten dead. Blood was everywhere and I, too, had been hit. In fact most of the officers had been wounded and it was actually Pfaffinger, our doctor (!), who dived the boat and commanded it back into Brest, where we could be taken off and treated. Typical of those times as well, despite our casualties there was no shortage of volunteers from the reserve pools of the 9th and 1st U-Flotillas to join the boat and take part in its next patrol!

"Pfaffinger was decorated for his actions, receiving the German Cross in Gold. Dönitz soon realized that the U-boat was not a good weapons platform for anti-aircraft missions and tried other tactics. Me, I was laid up in hospital while Klaus Hartmann took back his command. He sailed with *U441* against the Normandy invasion fleet and was lost with his entire crew."

Medical Officers aboard U-boats

"Our doctor not only was a good medical officer, but handy with a typewriter . . . and the radar detector."—Jürgen Oesten, *U861*

Trained medical personnel—as opposed to the medical duties handled by radio operators—were not necessarily part of a standard U-boat crew during World War II. It was deemed the *Kriegsmarine* medical service could not sustain the high casualty rate suffered by U-boats in combat. However, they were routinely at sea as part of the crew aboard long-distance and resupply U-boats.

Opium tablets supplied to U-boats for use as painkillers.

With larger U-boats heading into the South Atlantic and beyond, the illnesses suffered due to the heat and those exacerbated by long periods of confinement were thought by BdU to warrant a dedicated doctor. Also, should the task allotted to any particular boat be considered particularly hazardous, such as in the case of the seven dedicated Flak U-boats, they too would carry doctors. There seems little hard and fast pattern among the remainder of operational U-boats, and medical personnel were found on Type IX—and, less frequently, Type VII—U-boats throughout the War as was deemed necessary. During such service the doctor was officially classed as a non-combatant; he was not expected to undertake watch duties or any weapons-related tasks. However, many opted to fill their time with additional duties, such as assisting the radio crew, or more general onboard tasks that boosted the crew's morale, such as running an onboard newspaper.

Thermometer and its protective tube.

The more manual tasks, such as torpedo maintenance, were generally considered out of bounds, not only for obvious hygiene reasons but also because such tasks were assigned to enlisted men.

Those medical personnel that were part of the U-boat service came under the control of Dr Gerhard Lepel's Naval Medical Research Institute for U-boat Medicine (*Marine-ärztliches Forschungsinstitut für Uboot-medizin*), which was based in Carnac, near Lorient in France, between January 1942 and August 1944. Lepel had previously served as ship's doctor aboard the heavy cruiser *Gneisenau* before transferring to take control of the Carnac Institute.

As well as the obvious medical matters that required the attention of such crewmen, there was also a responsibility to cater for any vitamin pill requirements thought necessary for a particular cruise. While men of the German midget submarine service were provided with amphetamines, those of the U-boat arm were not. However, for certain particularly arduous long-distance voyages the provision of vitamins to supplement the men's diet became the responsibility of the medical officer. Once a week a small cellophane and aluminum-foil package containing 12 small cream-colored tablets was issued to each crewman. Additionally *Schoka-Kola*, a chocolate stimulant, was also given out as part of the food ration.

Aboard *U66* in May 1944 the lack of such supplies may indeed have contributed to the boat's destruction by enemy forces. To his horror, the inexperienced *Sanitätsmaat*, Wolf Loch, discovered that

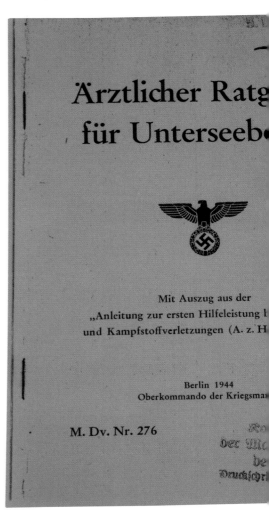

Ärztlicher Ratg für Unterseebe

Mit Auszug aus der „Anleitung zur ersten Hilfeleistung und Kampfstoffverletzungen (A. z. H

Berlin 1944
Oberkommando der Kriegsma

M. Dv. Nr. 276

Above: A booklet, "Medical Advice for U-boats: With extracts from 'Guidance for the first aid of accidents and weapon injuries' in part II."

Right: Minor injuries do not appear to have dampened the spirits of these men aboard U81. In the foreground is an Italian Breda machine gun, added at La Spezia to bolster their anti-aircraft defenses.

due to an error in loading at Lorient, the expected supply of vitamin pills in fact consisted of one small, inadequate bottle only. *U66* had left France on January 16 to operate off West Africa. By May, supplies of fuel and food were critically low and, exacerbated by the lack of vitamin supplements, the crew began to exhibit symptoms of scurvy, including lethargy and confusion. Attempts to rendezvous with resupply boats were thwarted by Allied pressure until a hunter-killer group centered on USS *Block Island* surprised the boat while it lay surfaced. The stuporous lookouts spotted the approaching aircraft too late, and the subsequent hunt destroyed *U66*. Twenty-four of the crew were killed.

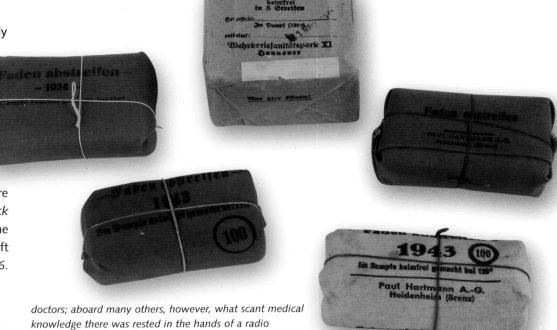

Right: *Standard-issue* Kriegsmarine *bandages. The degree to which illness or injury could be treated during combat patrols varied tremendously. Some U-boats carried trained doctors; aboard many others, however, what scant medical knowledge there was rested in the hands of a radio operator with little training or experience.*

Crossing the line (1)

Oberbootsmann Max Schley was "Number One" aboard *U861* on its long-range mission from Germany, via Norway to the Far East. As well as his usual responsibilities for the general well-being of boat and crew, he was also responsible for recommending promotions or crew rotations, and for the practical training of new men in all aspects of a sailor's life. His two assisting mates (*Bootsmannsmaate*) in turn looked after ammunition, administrative, and personnel issues of the seamen's division of the crew.

"Our commander was *Kptlt* Jürgen Oesten, who had already successfully commanded two U-boats and won the Knight's Cross; he came with most of his crew to *U861*. Most of the officers and non-commissioned officers

Above: *The crowded bridge watch aboard the Type IXD2 U861, heading for Penang, Malaysia, during late 1944.*
Right: Oberbootsmann Max Schley—*on top of the conning tower of U861—grasps the opportunity of his bridge watch to have a welcome smoke of his pipe.*

had combat experience, so we were confident. I had half a year on land behind me as, in August 1943, we finished our working up of the boat delivered from the Deschimag A.G. Weser yards in Bremen. (All of the engineering

crew under the command of the LI, *Kptlt (Ing)* Pankin, were well prepared as they had been with the boat the longest and even the seamen aboard had had six weeks of 'working-up' training time.) In theory and practice lessons most of our young men had been with the boat for a while and were ready for action by the time we were commissioning in September. Our boat was a Type IXD2, of about 1,200 tons. It was 93m [305ft] long with an 8m [26ft] beam. The two diesels could push it at 18 knots at full speed, and we could carry a total of 26 torpedoes. The weaponry consisted of four bow torpedo tubes and two stern ones, as well as a 10.5cm deck gun, two double-barrel 2cm Flak guns on the conning tower, and another single 3.7cm anti-aircraft gun as well. We were equipped with the *Bachstelze* gyro-copter and the crew totaled 64 men in all.

Above: *Evidence of the escalating technology war aboard U861—seen here is the parabolic radar detector known as the "Fliege," hand-turned by an operator on the bridge.*

"We left Germany on April 20, 1944, and then had a couple of days in Kristiansand South, Norway, which really was the calm before the storm—after that, the circus would begin. Our boat wasn't equipped with a *Schnorchel* so the plan was to sail submerged by day and surfaced by night so that we could recharge the batteries. The first night after we left Norway came soon enough. At about 21:00 hours the order came: 'Prepare to surface!' A radioman got ready to man his post at the radar detector mounted on top of the conning tower. As soon as the bridge was clear the first watch, with me among it, raced to our station. Our eyes adjusted rapidly to the darkness and with heavy binoculars we scanned the horizon, but we could see nothing. Well, that means we can get ourselves moving according to the Old Man [the Captain]. The diesels sprang into life and the boat leapt forward. The machinists also began to load the batteries, running off one of the engines. Approximately a quarter of an hour later the message came from the radioman: 'Detection on the bridge!' His equipment had picked up an enemy radar trace looking for us, and the reception was getting louder. What a damned

mess! This wouldn't help us at all. 'Everybody down!' orders the Old Man, and we leave the bridge, the boat then dipping below the surface.

"We want to stay down for about an hour and then head back up. The time passes exactly as it has a little while ago. So then we surface—and back down again. We carry on like this all night and the batteries steadily drain, as we can't give them any more juice. The following night we actually have no choice but to stay surfaced and as soon as we do so, the Flak guns are manned. We have to get some juice into the batteries, or the boat will be unable to function as we can't go for days underwater, and if we meet enemy ships we will have to dive. So we stay surfaced. We couldn't have made a crash dive with that many people on the bridge and *wintergarten* anyway. Our eyes scour the darkness and the gun crews stand at their weapons. If an aircraft comes now we will have to fight it out, and it will be hard to see in this darkness. And now suddenly the radar detector begins to chirp. 'Men,' says the Old Man, 'that really doesn't tell us anything we don't know. Radar detector off!' But the lack of audible warning doesn't make us any less nervous. Our batteries must

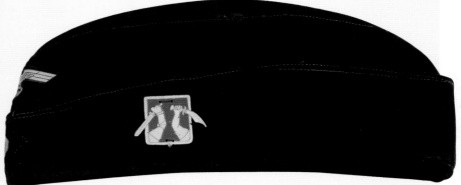

Above: *The U-boat seaman's* Bordmütze *(sidecap). This belonged to an enlisted man from U370; the boat's chosen emblem was based on a Finnish coat of arms.*
Left: *Standard-issue gear for the seaman branch—consisting of a three-quarter-length leather coat, rubberized hat, and warm woolen scarf.*

be full soon! The IIWO comes to the bridge. We are going to release two decoys—large balloons [called] Aphrodites—80cm [31in] in diameter and trailing aluminum strips that will attract the radar signals. So we inflate them and leave two trailing behind us, and so manage to escape attack. It was at home that we learnt to do this. We found aluminum strips after the massive bombing of Hamburg, and learnt that that was what the British had dropped to mess our radar up. So now we were happy to be doing the same to them.

"Finally, the batteries were full and we dived. We were going to slip between the Faroes and Ireland [although Schley refers to Ireland here he

Crossing the line (2)

must have meant Scotland] and into the North Atlantic. Naturally, we weren't able to move too fast as we were mainly submerged and could only manage about two nautical miles an hour. We managed a pair of surfaced miles every night which didn't take us far but at least cut some time off the trip. It took 70 days to get from Kiel to the 15° South latitude—with a *Schnorchel* we could have done it in half the time! Once we made the North Atlantic we were able to pick up the pace a little. And the men soon adapted to shipboard life and the new rhythms of day and night. With the differing parts of the ocean day became night. Lunch was at 24:00 hours. However, when we had been traveling submerged for most of the day it was impossible to eat well. The air was precious aboard the boat and we couldn't have steam produced by cooking ruining whatever fresh air there was.

"So, when we traveled like that all life on the boat became almost extinct. Apart from the men on the electric motors, those in the *Zentrale*, the helm and planesmen, all the others lay in their bunks. Here and there people played games, but by and large all was quiet. We had quite a large library aboard, but for 18 to 20 hours a day there was virtual silence. So we developed things to keep men occupied. We began to publish an onboard newspaper, largely run by the doctor and the Propaganda reporter we had on board. This entertained the men with its wit and humor, and everyone was welcome to contribute. On Sundays we had a 'concert,' where requests were played over the boat's loudspeakers from the gramophone in the radio room.

"But this voyage had its positive points. Ten to 12 hours' good sleep a day and we could almost forget the convoy battles. The boat was nice and peaceful, and we sailors were more than happy about that; also that we weren't constantly soaked in seawater on watch! And then when we surfaced the boat came alive. The bridge watch would race to their station, the diesels roar into life, the radioman tune into missed broadcasts while another manned the radar detector. Also, two men were assigned to empty buckets from aboard the boat. Our head [toilet] was normally under siege while we traveled surfaced but there was never enough time for nearly 70 men to use it before we dived. It was a noisy hand-pumped machine

Below: *"Crossing the line"—a ritual observed even in wartime. King Neptune and his "wife" Thetis initiate men crossing the Equator for the first time.*

Below: *The ceremony could take many forms, but generally involved a good deal of mess and cleaning up afterward.*

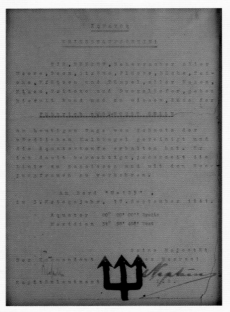

Above: *Certificate signed by "Neptune" and issued to* Fähnrich *Horst Selle, who crossed the line on September 17, 1941, aboard U125.*

and so when we traveled underwater those who had missed out got to use a large bucket situated within the head. Two 'Lords' would stand ready when we were surfacing and they would take the bucket between them, ask permission, and then head up to the bridge and throw the contents over the side.

"On June 23 we had reached the equator at the 27° West longitude. That afternoon over the loudspeaker came the message: 'Admiral Triton with his attendants have come aboard *U861* to inspect those ready to be baptized. All those men must leave their compartments now!' We were submerged so the men gathered in the officers' room. There, any thoughts of rank were forgotten and among those present were our doctor, the IWO, chief engineer, and the Propaganda reporter, all made ready to receive Triton's blessing. 'Attention! Eyes right!' and Admiral Triton and his two helpers entered the compartment. He took each officer by the hand and delivered his blessings. Good grief, they had outdone themselves and it was almost like peacetime. But then came the rest—a 2-cm [¾-in] diameter pill placed in the mouth that had to be swallowed. I can see it today, all our officers with these huge pills in their mouths. And the Admiral did his best to embarrass them, paying close attention to the fact that it was swallowed. Then he came to me. 'What? Fifteen war patrols you have behind you and they still let your dirty self run around on warships?' I believe that King Neptune had something special planned for me. So I too was given my pill to swallow and my God, it burnt my mouth, throat, and stomach for nearly an hour. Mustard, pepper, and engine grease were among the ingredients I could taste, but that wasn't all it contained. It wasn't finished yet either.

"The next day, the Holy Baptism took place. King Neptune himself came aboard, this time with his

attendants. And we all admired his 'wife,' Thetis, who was also present. She was built marvelously. I think the last time I had seen that was on the Reeperbahn [the red light district of Hamburg]! Neptune eventually seated himself on his throne in the *Zentrale*. The first to be baptized was our IWO, who came before Neptune. Then the baptism began. Man, oh man, it was harsh! He was dunked several times in bilge water—it went up his mouth and nose—and he was finally dragged groggily into the officers' mess, where he was given some Cognac. Eventually my turn came and I also had a ½ liter [1 pint] of bilge water sprayed into my mouth. I had stuff rubbed on my head and stank to high heaven afterward.

"And so the day ended and we headed further South, back toward the War. The doctor monitored those of us who could go outside to make sure we didn't get sunburn. The burning sun was beating down on our steel tube when we ran surfaced. The warm seawater also raised the interior temperature to 35ºC [95ºF], and up to 60ºC [140ºF] in the engine room. We seamen at least had the opportunity to get fresh air on the bridge watch. The high temperatures reduced men's appetites, although we had almost exhausted our fresh provisions anyway. And we began to hear about the other boats in our region. Many were lost. *U860*, commanded by FK Büchel, was sunk by aircraft near Cape Town. This boat was 14 days ahead of us. We had had a lot of contact with that boat and crew as they had also been commissioned in Bremen. Yes, the good times in the South Atlantic were over."

Above: Obermaschinist *Gerhard Leissner holding a microphone for Kptlt Friedrich Marks in U376, no doubt recording one of the oft-broadcast radio propaganda messages for the* Kriegsmarine. **Far left:** Funkmaat *Georg Seitz's crossing-the-line certificate, co-signed by the commander of the 9th U-Flotilla, Heinrich Lehmann-Willenbrock.*

Eastern Atlantic ops

Leutnant zur See Herbert Waldschmidt was the IIWO aboard Reinhard "Teddy" Suhren's *U564* in 1942, when the boat traveled to the Caribbean as part of Dönitz's onslaught in the Eastern Atlantic.

"I was posted to *U564* as my first operational boat in March 1942. I had already served in the training flotilla aboard the small Type II *U5*—so small we used to call them canoes! Anyway, I went to *U564* ready to go to war. It was a good crew: Suhren, Chief Engineer Ulrich Gabler, and First Watch Officer Ulf Lawaetz. They knew how to deal with men. I learnt a great deal from them, and altogether it was a happy ship.

"Unfortunately on my first patrol we sank the neutral Mexican tanker *Potrero del Llano* near Florida, and some of the crew were killed. Mexico then declared war—although I don't think it was solely for this reason. It was an accident; these things happen in war. On the next patrol we took a reporter out to film and photograph us at sea. His name was Haring and he slept in the quarters of the *Unteroffiziere* [Petty Officers]. We also had a trainee engineering officer, *Lt (Ing)* Hammermüller aboard to learn his trade, and he was quartered in my bunk—unless we were both off duty, in which case he was also in the *Unteroffiziere* compartment. As you know, Haring took many pictures and films of us, some of which ended up in the weekly cinema reports of Germany's war at sea.

"During that patrol we sank several ships, but we also intercepted a ship sailing alone. It had large Swedish flags on the side of the hull, which we could see through glasses [binoculars]. So, Teddy opted to intercept the ship and examine its papers. (This was in the days before aircraft made that kind of thing impossible.)

"Anyway, we made an approach to the Swede, with the gun crew at action stations. They looked ready to fire, but, in actual fact, we still had our torpedo-loading cradle out as we had been putting 'eels' into the bow room, and oughtn't to fire the gun in case we damaged the cradle. I signaled by lamp that the ship should stop and present papers, or risk being sunk. Teddy made the officers wear their caps so that we would look like a formidable military crew! They stopped and the Swedish captain came aboard by boat, while we kept the guns trained on his ship. The IWO, Lawaetz, was half Danish so he could talk easily with the man, though he understood German anyway. Teddy looked through the whole manifest of cargo and, sure enough, his papers were in order. So he went on his way—no contraband aboard. Apparently, another U-boat sank the ship later that year.

Above: L z S *Herbert Waldschmidt, IIWO of U564, seen as his boat approaches Brest harbor following two months on a patrol that extended as far as the Caribbean.* **Left:** *Wound badges in black and silver; the black one has lost its paint color. Three grades were awarded, for varying degrees of injury, with gold being the highest.*

"Also on that trip we received a message from BdU that *Obermaschinistenmaat* Fritz Hummel's wife had given birth. The message told of a 'new U-boat arrived with periscope,' meaning it was a boy! Dönitz did this kind of thing, which endeared him to us seamen, as we felt that he was personally interested in us and our welfare. We made a special presentation to Hummel, pasting a baby's face into the radio log. I think that Hummel must only have seen his son once, or maybe twice, as he was killed in June 1943 when *U564* was sunk off Cape Finistere. By then I had already left the boat.

"After leaving *U564*, in 1943 I was for a brief time in Bordeaux, before traveling to Memel and on to Gotenhafen, where, in May, I took command of the training U-boat *U146*. I think at that time, at the age of 21, I was the youngest commander in the *Kriegsmarine*. As it turned out, the War ended before I was in combat as a captain—two Type XXI boats that I was transferred to command were both destroyed by bombing. It wasn't until long after the War that I commanded the Type XXI— *Wilhelm Bauer*—for four years in the *Bundesmarine*."

Above left: *One of several photos made as* U564 *intercepted the Swedish freighter SS* Scania *on August 5, 1942.* U564 *gave chase, gun crew at Action Stations.*
Above right: *After the request to halt was heeded,* U564 *circled* Scania, *demanding to know what kind of cargo she was carrying.*

Above: *The Swedish First Officer boarding* U564 *with his ship's log. Once ship and cargo were verified as neutral,* Scania *was allowed to proceed.*

Far left: *An 88mm gun on a Type VII U-boat. Many were replaced by anti-aircraft Flak guns after 1942.*

Aboard *U802* Maschinenobergefreiter Karl-Heinz Wahnig witnessed first hand the work of an onboard doctor during the boat's first patrol to Nova Scotia in April 1944, after the serious wounding of a petty officer:
"On April 11 we had had a lot of air attacks and were very badly damaged. The depth sounder had broken down, but we had a gadget called an 'echo load' [a small explosive charge] which you throw overboard. You measure the depth by the time it takes for the sound to come back as it explodes on hitting the seabed. A seaman petty officer on board was in charge of the echo load and while he was handling it, the canister with all the charges exploded, injuring his face and left hand. We had to dive down and settle on the seabed so that our doctor, Dr Rudolf Neumann, could operate. First, he had to amputate his finger as he was losing a lot of blood. Then, five days later, complications arose with the petty officer's eyes. Although a doctor carried surgical instruments, he didn't have an implement to take an eye out. So we had to make one ourselves, in the engine room, from a brass rod. It was the shape of a pair of scissors with two bars across each end, so that he could get right behind the eye and take the left one out to check if there were any complications there. It was successful and later Neumann received the Iron Cross First Class for his achievement."

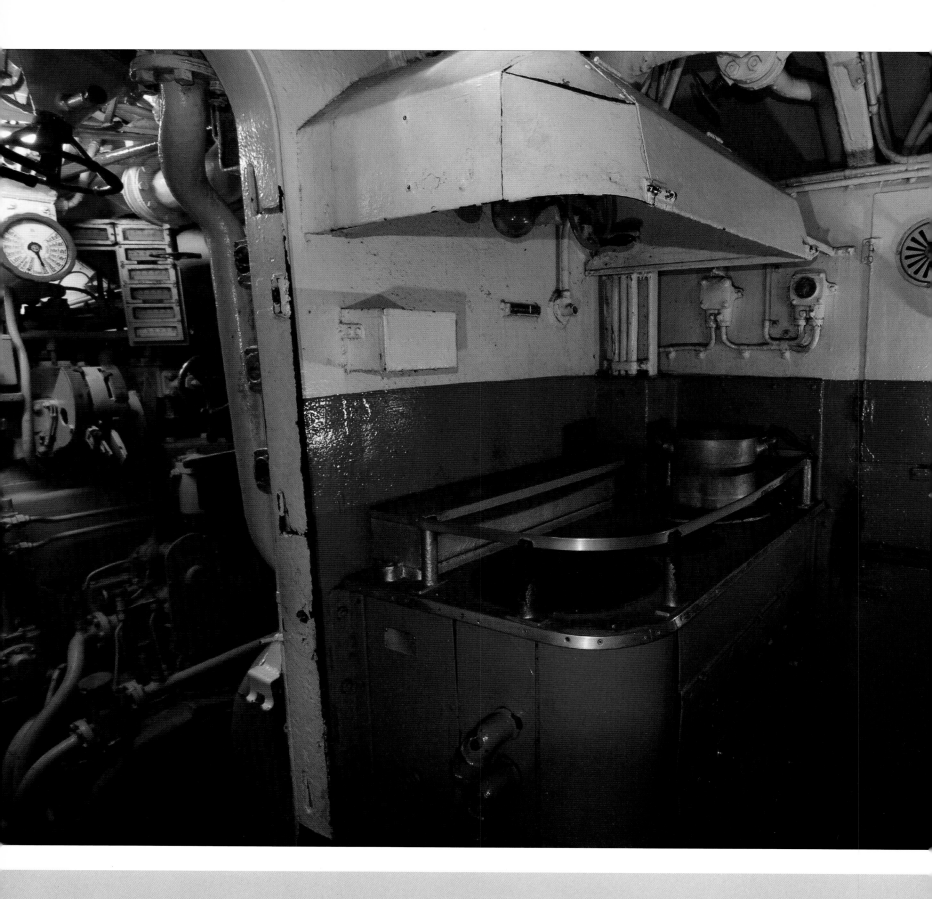

The Galley

**"The food? The food was good—as long as you liked
the taste of diesel."**—Jürgen Oesten, *U106*

Interestingly, despite the terrible reputation of moldy food permeated throughout with the rank taste of diesel oil, the *Kriegsmarine*'s U-boat service was supplied with some of the best rations issued to *Wehrmacht* troops. Scurvy—a potentially life-threatening condition caused by vitamin C deficiency—had long been the bane of seafarers the world over and the close attention to detail taken by the U-boat service in provisioning its men at sea was remarkable. No less remarkable was the lack of actual design effort put into the storage of such foodstuffs in an operational Type VIIC U-boat.

While in harbor the crewmen ate in extreme comfort, with little evidence of rationing until the closing stages of the War. At sea, the boats carried a great variety of food-stuffs with which to feed their crews. However, it was the storage of such food that caused the greatest problems. There was little by way of dedicated food storage areas included in the design of a Type VIIC, and even less by way of refrigeration. Spoilage of fresh provisions was a common problem—particularly in equatorial regions, where the ambient temperature could become almost unbearable inside the steel hull, submerged or not.

The galley itself was located aft of the petty officers' room, on the port side of the hull. There, the cook was equipped with a two-burner electric stove with small oven, refrigerator, self-heating soup kettle, provision lockers, and an enamel sink with hot and cold fresh water as well as hot salt water. Opposite, on the starboard side, was the battery switching room and aft head; the latter

Left: *The galley aboard U995. A small food storage locker, with adjustable vent, is situated above an equally small refrigerated compartment to the side of the electric cooking stove. The diesel engine room can be seen through the doorway.*

generally piled high with provisions at the beginning of a voyage. The actual cupboard storage space provided for provisions was meager, both in the galley and in the locker situated forward of the petty officers' quarters, and tended to be taken up with non-perishables. Large sides of hams, sausages, and other preserved meats were generally stowed between the forward torpedo tubes and also overhead in the control room. These spaces were considered relatively out of the way and were regarded as good places for long-term storage. Bread was stored in the forward torpedo room and electric motor room in hammocks, or some other form of netting. Fresh meat, vegetables, and fruit were stored in the tiny refrigerator and pantry, along with whatever supplies of cream the boat carried. The provision of alcohol differed from boat to boat—some captains maintained a strictly "dry" ship, while others allowed some beer and rum on board, although it was strictly rationed by the captain himself.

The cook aboard a U-boat—known to the crew as the *Smutje*—had no watch duties. While a *Smutje* would occasionally help with artillery or torpedo work, his primary task was to cook for the crew manning the U-boat around the clock. Provisioning the boat, however, was not within the *Smutje*'s remit: the IIIWO, the boat's navigator (*Obersteuermann*), doubled as ship's quartermaster, being responsible for the accounting for—and loading of—foodstuffs, as well as its storage within the hull. Where different foods were stored was dictated by three main criteria: the food had to be secure, so that it would not come loose during enemy action; it needed to be evenly distributed, so it would not disturb the boat's trim; and it could not obstruct any hatches, valves, or vital systems, which had to remain accessible at all times.

The daily consumption and concurrent change of internally stored weight was a matter the cook and IIIWO needed to confer on, the IIIWO in turn liaising with the boat's Chief Engineer in order to calculate any readjustment of trim. The only other task given over to the cook was to report any problems with the boat's stern hatchway positioned above the galley. The boats' cooks were not necessarily chosen on the basis of ability for the job before enlistment within the *Kriegsmarine*. They attended a brief cooking course, and were then assigned to their U-boat. Thus, the culinary prowess of any given *Smutje* could differ wildly. U-boat commanders blessed with a particularly gifted cook often tried to keep him, doing their best to prevent him being rotated to assignments on other boats.

Menus aboard ship were carefully constructed so as to provide as balanced a diet as possible. Breakfasts normally comprised coffee or cocoa, milk soup with crisp bread (*Knäckebrot*), rusk (*Zwieback*) with jam, honey, butter, or eggs. Lunch would consist of some form of soup, potatoes, cooked meat, and vegetables, and also fruit, while dinner generally included sausages or canned fish, cheese, liver sausage (pâté), bread, and coffee, tea, or chocolate.

While returning U-boats often rendezvoused with those still on patrol to hand over any uneaten and no longer required stores, following the development and deployment of large Type XIV supply U-boats, combat boats were able to replenish not only ammunition but also fresh foodstuffs while at sea. Aboard the so-called *Milchkuh* supply boats there was a bakery capable of producing up to 40 loaves of bread per day. They were also equipped with large refrigerators, in which each item was strictly marked to insure that nothing perished before being transferred to a combat boat. Indeed, *U462* reported that it baked 700 loaves of fresh bread during a single patrol. The *Milchkuh* supply boats enabled the U-boats to extend their war into the southern Atlantic and Indian oceans.

Page right, clockwise from top left: Kriegsmarine cutlery, identifiable by the stamped eagle above the letter "M," for "Marine"; the galley's sink, with taps for the different types of water available; the filter for extracting drinking water from desalinated seawater; a standard-issue Kriegsmarine tea towel; the soup kettle aboard U995—this would have been in almost constant use, as soup was a mainstay of the U-boat crew's diet, especially once foods began to perish.

The water supply

The duration of an operational patrol depended to a large degree on maintaining sufficient supplies of fuel, ammunition, food, and, crucially, water. The galley of a U-boat was thus provided with four different grades of water, each with its own labeled tap (left to right): washing water; filtered drinking water; warm salt water; and fresh drinking water, which was held in dedicated storage tanks.

Kombüse und Reserve-WC

Der Koch ("Smut") ist
auf jedem Schiff ein
besonders wichtiger
Mann, auf einem U-Boot
dazu ein Künstler. Auf
engstem Raum wurde

für 56 Mann mehrmals
täglich gekocht. Im
Reserve-WC waren
Lebensmittel gelagert
– es war also
zuerst unbenutzbar.

Trinkwasserfilter

Kriegsmarine   Kriegsmarine

Kriegsmarine   Kriegsmarine

Spanish try-outs

Hans-Rudolf Rösing took one of the first Type VII U-boats into the Atlantic ocean during the time of the Spanish Civil War, in the 1930s. Despite the covert presence of two U-boats that actually fought on the side of the Spanish Nationalists (they sunk a Republican submarine, *C3*, on December 12, 1936), Rösing's mission was of a peaceful nature: to test the new boats in the open ocean.

"When I captained *U35* in 1937, I—and Looff in *U28*—made the first Atlantic cruises of the new U-boats. At the time we were to be sent to the Spanish Civil War but when we were equipped and ready the war was virtually over, so we were sent to the Azores instead. We made the first expedition in really heavy weather. We had a Force 11 to 12 and we found out what excellent sea-going ships these submarines were. And when it was too wet we could go down and relax.

"Of course, as usual I was seasick. I used to be seasick for the first two days in the cruise, but later I was okay. Normally I never did anything about it, but in the War, of course, I took medicine.

"Combined with the trials of the boats themselves there was an opportunity to check the weapons and also that the provisions stored aboard the boat were provided in their correct quantity, that they were usable, and that their placement was alright. It was important that the amount of fresh food could last for as long as possible and that the preserved foodstuffs were properly prepared before we had to rely on them."

Kptlt Werner Hartmann, too, undertook a Spanish voyage as commander of the Type I U-boat *U26* between May and June 1937, also to evaluate all aspects of operational patrolling. His findings revealed certain shortcomings in the onboard provisions.

"Fresh provisions were delivered in good condition, but due to the time of year it was possible to provide fresh food for only four days and some things that had been ordered could not be delivered. There was only sufficient freshly canned meat for ten days, although this still featured on the menu for day 42. After 12 days we had run out of all fresh food. A number of cans developed bubbles and the pressure became so great that some of them split open. The bad air coming out remained in the storage area for three days and in the rest of the boat for two days . . . Too much cheese was provided. Eighty tine of Camembert were ordered but these arrived in wooden boxes and the smell was somewhat unbearable. The eggs lasted until the last day without too many losses. The egg boxes were restacked every third day.

"The 300 hard-baked loaves kept for four weeks without a great deal of waste, but 200 would have been sufficient. The bread was stored in hammocks and it was taken up into the open in port to have the mold scraped off. Despite this, some 100 loaves had to be discarded. The delivered potatoes were good. Since they were stored in too hot a place, they were redistributed to other areas and once in port they were taken up onto the upper deck to dry out in the sun . . . About 150kg [330lb] had to be thrown away because they were unusable.

"There was not much use for flour and the sacks in which it was delivered had a tendency to develop mold fairly quickly. There was ample

Top: *Loading supplies aboard U617 in the Italian U-boat port of La Spezia, March 1943. Behind the two U-boat men is the Italian cruiser* Taranto.

Above: *Stores being loaded into the bow compartment of a Type VIIC. Behind the hatch are stacked loaves of bread, for storage in bow hammocks.*

Below: *A small Kriegsmarine-stamped dish, probably used for salt at mealtimes.*

rice, which kept well. There was plenty of canned fruit aboard. The cans of blood sausage and corned beef had a guarantee date stamped on them of January 1, 1937, and they were delivered on May 3, 1937. Thirty cans of sprouts turned out to be 30 cans of cauliflower.

"The men received butter, canned fish, and cheese every day and sausage every other day so that there was plenty of variation in the diet. Lauer [the *Smutje*] made a great effort in the galley and his performance was good—no matter how rough the sea was or what other problems occurred."

Maschinenobergefreiter Mengelberg was aboard one of the Type I U-boats, U26, for six of its seven war patrols during 1939 and 1940.

"I sailed in *U26*, an old-type sub and, yes, we had a small refrigerator for small perishable goods only. Bread had been skin-roasted and was stored in net-hammocks in the electric motor room, which was the warmest. All canned food found its place in the bilge of the diesel room. Fresh supplies, such as vegetables, lasted for only about one week, and that was all. We were two sailors to a bunk, and were doing that for up to six weeks, and that bunk was damp from the sweat drops coming from the wall of the pressure hull above your bunk. All we received was half a cup of water to clean your teeth every second day, one set of underwear—and that was the one you had on yourself—the tiny locker was about 51x20x13cm [20x8x5in]. All I had in there was what we called 'Tyty,' a second-grade perfume we used here and there to change from 'sweat-diesel' odor to 'Tyty'—that smell lasted not a hell of a long time. Yes, and we even had a mouse in the boat for five patrols, but on the last patrol the mouse had left the boat. In all six patrols I was never given beer or rum, or any other type of alcoholic drink. After eight days our fresh food was consumed and then we often ate direct out of a can—saves washing dishes because water was there for cooking only and perhaps the half a cup of water to clean your teeth. Vitamin tablets were given against scurvy—I took them because I knew I had to.

"The only other question that often pops up is [about] the Adolf Hitler picture. It was mounted in such a position across from the commander's hideaway on the wall that one had to look up to notice it. It wasn't a big deal and was only really mounted there by order of the government—we were not all in favor of Adolf or the Nazis, as you might believe."

Above, far left: *Corned beef hash—made with corned beef supplies from the Emery Food Company—being prepared aboard a 9th U-Flotilla U-boat. The cook is wearing British-style battledress fatigues. His flotilla is identifiable by the "Laughing Sawfish" cap badge.*

Left: *Hans-Rudolf Rösing, pictured in 1940 when he was captain of U48. Rösing entered naval service in 1925, becoming one of Dönitz's first volunteer U-boat officers.*

The daily diet

As U-boats had so little dedicated food storage space, the question of where to stow the provisions was a problematic one—particularly when it came to the fresh foods, a wide variety of which were included in the U-boat men's diet. Reinhard Suhren of *U564* explained the difficulties: "The diet in the first eight days was quite good—for instance, we had a lot of fresh vegetables and fruit, and so on. In fact everything fresh was used up. The galley was situated between the non-commissioned officers' room and the fuel room. In the galley, the cooker was on the port side while on the starboard side was a toilet, piled up with fresh vegetables, fruit, meat, etc. First of all, it is not very nice to have a toilet in the galley, but on the other hand 46 men to only one [toilet] situated in a different part of the boat is just not enough!

"Mind you, a lot of boats used the toilet in the galley as a provisions room. When all of the fresh food was used up, we turned to canned food. On the whole our provisions were very good, in fact we had everything—although it all tasted of diesel oil.

"The biggest problem was the bread. We had placed it in a hammock so that plenty of air could get to it, but after a while it used to go stale and then moldy so that it looked just like rabbits—white, furry rabbits—

because it was covered in so much mildew. We just removed as much of it as possible and ate it. When a journey lasted longer than four weeks, the food became a problem and to keep the crew in good health was not easy. My longest journey as commander lasted three months and in that time we stopped for diesel, which we received from a tanker, and we were also restocked with provisions."

Interestingly, it is not just German veterans who can recall the diet and conditions aboard a wartime U-boat. The master of SS *Empire Starling*, Eric Monckton, was taken prisoner aboard *U163* on November 21, 1942, after his ship had been sunk east of Barbados. On *U163*, he experienced the hardships of U-boat life for himself: "My first meal was some hour or so after I had been taken on board, and it consisted of a soup made from canned vegetables, cold meat sausage with potatoes, canned fruit, and black bread from airtight cans and also butter. The plates used were the usual wooden platters of the Germans.

"Throughout the whole of my passage on *U163*, which was a large Type IXC U-boat, the food consisted of soups, sausages, liver sausage, canned fruits, and vegetables. We got meat later on when the *U163* was replenished near the Bay of Biscay by a submarine tanker, and then it was only sufficient to last for two days. When I arrived on board there were some potatoes, about half a ton [500kg] at the most, stored underneath the navigating table in the control room under the conning tower. These potatoes lasted only a few days as the Germans did not appear to know how to preserve them. When they started to go bad, they bucketed them on to the harbor deck while they were proceeding on the surface, washed them in salt water, and then restowed them in the locker. Within two days there was the smell of rotten fish about the potatoes; they had all gone bad.

"The other food was all canned and the products mostly of Portugal, Italy, France, and Denmark, to whom the crew used to refer to as 'our *Kammeraden*' but in my estimation of the first two countries, just rats to be trading with a country that was doing so much harm and whose ideals were so foreign to them.

"The small galley for cooking the meals was forward of the officers' quarters and was of very limited space but

Left and far left: Food took up valuable space aboard U-boats. Torpedo men (far left) reloading tubes in the bow room on U673 share their space with a mesh hammock loaded with bread, while the helmsman's position (left) is garlanded with sausages.

fitted with electric stove and oven, electric water boiler, and the usual pantry washing equipment. The cook was supposed to be very good at cooking and baking, but he had little opportunity to exhibit his knowledge as all he did was to open the cans of products and make the contents into soup.

"Breakfast was served at about 7 o'clock and consisted of a milk soup, coffee, and cookies or bread and jam. The bread was of two kinds—light and dark—carried in hermetically sealed cans, round in shape and about 10cm [4in] in diameter by 23cm [9in] in length. This bread kept very well—though it was a little dry.

"The food on *U163* might have been good at the start of her patrol, but while I was on board—except for a few days after we were supplied by the submarine tanker—everything was canned food after the potatoes had gone bad. I did not even see any egg powder and fresh eggs had long since been eaten up. The preservation of stores was a thing that from the commander downward no one knew the slightest thing about. Even opened cans of meat, fish, and vegetables were left for long periods with their contents remaining in the can and it was a source of wonder to me that there were not any cases of food poisoning among officers and crew.

"The *U163* was alive with cockroaches—a filthy, repulsive-looking insect—but no attempt was ever made to reduce their number or even to keep them in check. They crawled over everything and everywhere, food being left about for them to tackle. The many small sliding panel compartments or lockers in the wood lining of the interior of the submarine that were used for the stowage of canned food were alive with these cockroaches and they were a great nuisance when sleeping or resting."

Above: *The enlisted men aboard U564 at mealtime were unable to use the small folding tables provided in the bow room because of the torpedoes and food sacks stored there.*

Above left: *Though slightly larger and located in the forward half of the U-boat— between the officers' and warrant officers' rooms—the galley space aboard Type IX U-boats was as cramped and busy as aboard the Type VIIC.*

Left: *Typical* Kriegsmarine *cutlery, with the distinguishing stamped eagle and letter "M," seen here on the knife handle. Each crewman had his own utensils, as limited space in the galley did not allow for storage of an entire crew's cutlery.*

Boredom—and mealtimes!

Among the captured items taken from *U505* by the US Navy in 1944 was a personal diary believed to have been written by the only man killed during the boat's capture—*Oberfunkmaat* Gottfried Fischer. In the diary he recorded the boredom, the arduous conditions—and the meals that marked each passing day:

"14th day. It is 14 days today since we departed from the base. Throughout the entire period we have seen neither the sky nor the sun. The days go by slowly. We have finally crossed the dangerous area of maximum air threat—the Bay of Biscay. Hence was our transit: we hardly had time to breathe some fresh air and charge our batteries, and down below we went again. For the past three days we have been experiencing rough seas, sea state 3–6, high swell, and wind. The crockery is flying all around the inside of the boat, and an escape breathing apparatus nearly hit my head. It is a relief to submerge in this kind of weather. Miraculously, even though we had pudding, apple compôte, and other sweet things, everything stayed inside me. Small wonder, after all, our ancestors were all seafarers!

Above: The small galley area was immediately astern of the control room aboard a Type IIA U-boat.

"April 1: Tonight, while we ran on the surface, the sea was exceptionally vicious. Sea state 6–7. The boat rolls and pitches even at depths of 7–20m [23–66ft]. And then we sit (or rather stand) in our radio room and monitor our equipment, and fret about whether the enemy has already detected us. It is tiresome work. We are on a south-westerly heading of 120°.

"The warmer climate is already beginning to make itself felt. How is it going to get once we cross the equator in a few days?

"April 3: Mum's birthday. It's 12:30 hours and I've just wolfed down a cutlet, which would not have gone down well, had we been on the surface. What are you having today? A decent birthday dinner, I hope. *Grüne Klösse* [green dumplings—a regional German specialty]. We were treated with fresh rolls today, as if to mark the occasion; three per person. Have the flowers I have asked for been delivered? We've spent the past two nights on the surface. During that time, with the heavy sea going, I was unable to eat anything at all . . . It is always lunch I have to skip because we've turned the day into night, and vice versa. So, when it is noon at home, we're submerged and we call it midnight over here. Due to the heavy seas, which meet us head on, we've made only slow progress, even though we run on the surface 12 hours every day. Our area of operations is still unknown; we don't know whether we're bound for America or Africa. The mystery should be solved within the next few days, once we get our instructions by wireless.

"Easter Sunday, 21:00 hours: We have just finished our coffee break. Plum cakes were made to celebrate the holiday. In spite of the Sunday feeling the atmosphere is a bit tense. The officers and warrant officers had buttercream with their pastry. And I thought there were supposed to be no exceptions on a U-boat on combat patrol! Three days ago we rendezvoused with *U123*. As it was on its way back, they took on board everybody's letters to their families. Our radar detector has been broken for two days. Troubleshooting. To wrap up the day I spent nearly four hours repairing [the equipment] and sweating. We have been on a 180° heading for a few days now. The sea has calmed down but the heat has become more intense.

"April 14: It is four weeks today since we left base. What a thankless task, and we have got another three months to go! We have been assigned our area of operations by wireless today: the West-African Gold Coast. We're on a heading of 210° with the Cape Verde Islands just on our beam. Unfortunately we're not going anywhere close to the equator. I would have loved to take part in a crossing-the-line ceremony, even though I'm certain Neptune would not have shown any mercy with us. Fortunately, we were able to fix our radar detector again—after four long night shifts. Rations have been reduced drastically. We have already gone three evenings without sausage. They say that provisions have to last for a total of 17 weeks, even though we only took on provisions (including fresh groceries) for 14 weeks. That's how it is being a poor '*U-Boots-Schwein*,' as they call us. Yesterday we logged our 200th hour of surface transit during this patrol."

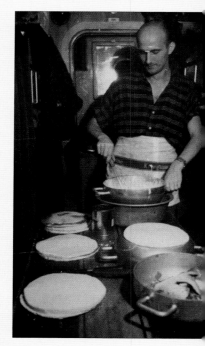

Right: *On the way to the officers' mess (top); Funkmaat Willi Anderheyden—though not the boat's cook—gives baking a try aboard U564.*

Above: *Porcelain bowls, plates, and mugs used on the U-boats. Impractical in heavy weather and depth-charge attacks alike, the breakage rate was high!*

Right: *The* Smutje *aboard U281, Matrosengefreiter Bruno Filipiak, seen at work. The movable ladder was used when the galley hatch was open.*

Hans Goebeler was also aboard *U505* and had fond memories of the boat's cook and his prowess with the kettle and hot plate:

"Around midnight Anton 'Toni' Kern, our boat's cook, would come to the bridge with his steaming pot of *Mittelwächter*, a much-welcomed mixture of very strong coffee laced with rum. He had to guard the pot like a hawk since the tasty black brew was very much desired by everyone in the crew, whether on watch or not.

"Toni and I became good friends. I remember the time he tried to make a big pot of tea for the crew. Most Germans are coffee drinkers and so Toni had not been trained to make tea during his four-week cook's course in U-boat school. In his ignorance, he used the same measure of tea leaves as one would for coffee. He then boiled the leaves until the tea was as black as motor oil. The stuff tasted bitter as poison when we tried to drink it! Well, *Kptlt* Löwe's mother was Dutch, so the skipper was a big tea drinker. Naturally, he demanded it be properly brewed. It was very amusing to watch the skipper hovering over the stove like a patient old aunt, instructing a very embarrassed Toni on the intricacies of tea-making."

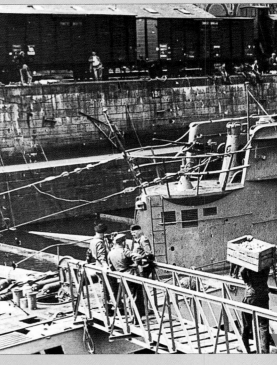

Planning the menu

Menus for use on operational voyages were carefully worked out before the boat was loaded to insure the correct supplies were taken aboard. Care was taken not only to provide the balanced diet necessary for the crew's health, but also to allow some variety in the food—for mealtimes were a highlight of the day for the men who had to live together in cramped confinement for weeks at a time. For example, a Type IXC U-boat catering for a crew of 55 men for 12 weeks at sea would take onboard 27,740lb [12,583kg] of food and drink. Included within this total were:

494lb [224kg] fresh and cooked meats (recommended stored in refrigerator),

238lb [108kg] sausages,

4,807lb [2,180.5kg] canned or preserved meat,

334lb [151.5kg] preserved fish,

3,858lb [1,750kg] fresh potatoes (recommended stored in bow and stern rooms, or in crates within the *zentrale*),

3,428lb [1,555kg] other vegetables (recommended stored in bow room and refrigerator),

917lb [416kg] (13 boxes) of lemons (recommended stored in bow room),

661lb [300kg] fresh fruit,

595lb [270kg] (ten boxes) of other fresh eggs (recommended stored in bow and stern rooms),

1,005lb [456kg] fresh bread (recommended stored in bow, stern, and electric motor rooms),

1,455lb [660kg] (300 cans) of canned bread,

110lb [50kg] butter,

110lb [50kg] fresh cheese,

143lb [65kg] canned cheese,

132lb [60kg] coffee and ersatz coffee,

7lb [3kg] tea,

1,728lb [784kg] (28 boxes) of milk.

These supplies had been calculated alongside a menu for the cook to work to. Again, an example from that provided for a Type IXC U-boat, *U518*, this time planning for six weeks at sea, showed the following daily dishes, selected to mark the beginning of each week at sea:
All breakfasts—coffee, cocoa, milk soup with crackers and crispbread, jam, honey, butter or eggs on demand.

Above: *Fishing for sharks, particularly near the equator, was one way of bulking up rations aboard combat U-boats.*

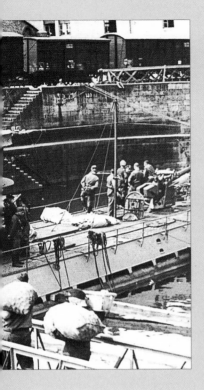

Far right: *Constant catering created a detritus of dishes and utensils, collected in large trays for washing in the cramped galley.*

Day 1:
Midday meal—Soup, mashed potatoes, liver, fresh fruit.
Evening meal—Spicy blood sausage, smoked meat, bread, butter, coffee.

Day 7:
Midday meal—Fried sausage, potatoes, gravy, cabbage, fresh fruit.
Evening meal—Herring salad, cooked beef and pork sausage (*Jagdwurst*), bread, butter, tea.

Day 14:
Midday meal—Soup, spinach with eggs, potatoes, stewed fruit.
Evening meal—Ham, radishes, bread, butter, and rosehip juice.

Day 21:
Midday meal—Soup, macaroni with ham, sauce, pudding with juice.
Evening meal—Noodle soup with beef, chilled ham, bread, butter, and apple juice.

Day 28:
Midday meal—Potato salad, scrambled eggs, mixed stewed fruit.
Evening meal—Macaroni with ham, tomato sauce, rose-hip juice.

Above left: *Food crates are broken open dockside in order to transfer each item individually through narrow hatchways.*
Above right: *The* Smutje *at work in his small galley.*

Day 35:
Midday meal—Soup, onion beef (*Zwiebelfleisch*), potatoes, gravy, vegetables, pudding with juice.
Evening meal—Ham, hard-boiled eggs, bread, butter, cocoa.

Day 42:
Midday meal—Bean soup with beef and pork.
Evening meal—Free composition according to available provisions (last day of voyage).

Resupply at sea

Oberbootsmann Max Schley was the "Number One" aboard *U861*, a large Type IXD2 U-boat headed for the Far East during April 1944.

"As well as our crew of 64 men we had two extra heads for the journey. The first was our medical officer and the second a man from the Propaganda Company. The latter, a *Sonderführer*, came aboard with a mountain of equipment. But somehow we made it all fit and we were soon ready to get going. Our food supplies were stuffed into every corner, nook, and cranny aboard the boat. And despite his strictly worked-out plans, I was still amazed by the way that our *Smutje* came up with something different each day.

"Our outward voyage from Germany was broken by two days in Norway at Kristiansand South. Besides other fresh provisions brought aboard was a large barrel full of herrings. But the taking of this barrel became quite difficult as it was extremely heavy and had such a wide circumference it wouldn't fit easily down any hatch. Our entry hatches were not that large. So eventually by rocking it backward and forward we managed to get the barrel with our little 'outboard comrades' [*Aussenbordkameraden*]—I mean the herrings—through the tower hatch and into the *zentrale*. So pickled herrings began to dominate our menu, as did their smell the boat. I have to mention here that this barrel full of herrings has remained etched in my memory like an extra crewman."

The deployment of the *Milchkuh* supply U-boats extended the time combat units— particularly Type VIICs—could remain at sea. *Obersteuermann* Heinz Theen of *U653* relied on them when BdU ordered him on a mission off Guiana in June 1943, although often it was solely fuel that he required.

"We began our seventh war patrol on June 10, 1943, destination the Caribbean. In May 1943 the death of U-boats in the North Atlantic had begun, mainly due to aircraft. They were everywhere and were making it impossible for the 'Nazi U-boats' to sink enemy shipping. When we were leaving there was an existing order from BdU in force for all U-boats to travel in groups of four or five, traveling by night underwater and during the day on the surface. This new tactic had come about because too many boats had been bombed and lost in the Bay of Biscay, the reasoning being that at least in daylight we could see them coming.

"Our captain, *Kptlt* Feiler, was the designated leader of a group of three boats: *U653*, *U564* under command of *Oblt z S* Fiedler who had replaced 'Teddy' Suhren, and *U185* commanded by *Kptlt* Maus, and they all obeyed the new directive. However, on June 14 our three boats were attacked by a Sunderland. The aircraft—and these things were huge and well armored—sank *U564* and then came after us. Before he came in to bomb us he was hit by gunfire from *Obermaat* Scholz. Yes, of course it was the Third Watch on the bridge! After *U564* had been sunk both *U653* and *U185* continued toward the front. *U185* was later sunk by aircraft on August 24.

"We topped up with fuel from the supply boat *U462*, the fuel we received allowing us to reach our destination within the Caribbean. Today

Above: Matrosengefreiter *Walter Skots*, the cook aboard U604, loads provisions through the open galley hatch—this was rarely, if ever, opened at sea due to the risk of swamping.

Right: U564 *takes diesel from* U463, *a Milchkuh supply U-boat, mid-Atlantic in 1942. A hose trails from* U463 *as both boats travel slowly.*

it is a desired vacation destination, but we were there for another reason! We went there to sink ships. But nothing—no ships were to be seen and aircraft chased us about day and night so that we always had to dive. We could hear ships over the hydrophone but had absolutely no success. It was miserable and many of the crew came down with tropical fever. Finally, in August the fuel and food were virtually exhausted so the order to head home came from BdU. But which boat was going to supply us with fuel? Several U-tankers had been destroyed at sea. We were told by BdU to take fuel from *U525* but she never showed up as she had been sunk on August 11. *U653* then received a short signal from BdU to head for quadrant DF91 and there to replenish from *U847*, a large Type IXD2 that was on its way to the Far East.

"In the gray morning light of August 28 we met *U847* and immediately began taking on fuel. About our ration state, *Kommandant* Feiler assumed that we could do without taking on more rations after I, as the Quartermaster responsible for provisions and the menu like all *Obersteuermänner*, announced to him that we would be able to get along okay with the supplies aboard, even if it took work using the canned meals available to be cooked by the *Smutje*. Food would have to be shuttled over in dinghies and that took time, so the

captain was able to make a fast resupply with only taking fuel. That probably saved our lives as aircraft sank *U847* later that day. *U653* entered Brest harbor on September 14 after 97 days at sea. Our boat was a Type VIIC. We had lost many friends in the boats. When we celebrated we couldn't feel any more joy. Maybe it was the demands on our nerves, or perhaps just hearing of the loss of so many boats from the 1st and 9th U-Flotillas based in Brest in the last three months. The captain, *Obermaschinisten*, myself, and ten of the crew had made seven patrols, totalling 434 days at sea. For us, replacements arrived before the eighth patrol, which ultimately had no success. During their ninth patrol the boats were sunk by the sloops HMS *Starling* and *Wild Goose* in the North Atlantic after being bombed by aircraft from the escort carrier HMS *Vindex*. There were no survivors."

Far left: *Sausages are strung from the bracing crosspiece of the forward torpedo loading hatch aboard U37.*

Below left: *While cooking was the domain of the* Smutje, *more mundane tasks, such as peeling potatoes, were shared out among the enlisted men off-duty in the bow room.*
Below right: *Visible behind the cook's head is another important piece of galley equipment—a coffee grinder.*

Heading for disaster

Wolfgang Frank, who later commanded France's *Kriegsmarine* Propaganda service, accompanied the noted "Ace" Günther Prien and his boat *U47* on a patrol during 1940.

"In the morning I was awakened at 7am by an impingement of smell and sound: the aroma of fresh coffee and the radio voice of a bulletin. I got up and went to the wardroom, where the luckless steward was having his usual struggle with the crockery. Before breakfast everyone took his turn to use the heads and have his morning clean-up. The air was fragrant with the scent of Colibri, the submariners' favorite brand of eau-de-cologne. Then we sat down to coffee, bread, and butter and jam. [However, within days this peaceful life was soon ruined by the onset of harsher North Atlantic weather:]

"It really is more than a joke. At breakfast this morning again butter, coffee, milk, liver sausage, two kinds of jam, bread, sugar, rubber boots, and leather gear were mingled in a fantastic heap with official papers on the coconut matting runner, and Hans-Joachim Bothmann was dancing around as if he had been stung by a hornet—the coffee pot had been spilled right into his lap. Luckily he was wearing his leather gear or else he would have been badly scalded. For my part I am sitting at the mess table hanging on for dear life. At one moment the edge of the table crushes my ribs as the boat rolls to starboard, and the next I am lying flat on my back on the settle as she rolls in the opposite direction."

Opposite the galley was the small compartment housing the stern head. Later in the War, some boats were equipped with special high-pressure heads that could be used at greater depths than the old-style models— but to operate the mechanism, a complex set of instructions had to be followed carefully. In April 1945 the brand-new Type VIIC *U1206* left Norway on a patrol, only to be lost on April 14. As FdU West, Hans-Rudolf Rösing was responsible for issuing orders to the boat; but it was only after the War that he discovered the true cause of her demise:

"The stern head in boats that had two, like the Type VIIs and IXs, was generally used for food storage until it had been eaten and was free to use [for its true purpose]. That could make life somewhat difficult in the early days of a patrol like mine aboard *U48*. All those men and only one head. At least in the early days before aircraft became a problem it was possible to relieve oneself over the side when running surfaced, either just standing there, or even using a small seat! However, when submerged the head could not be used below 25m [82ft] as the water pressure outside was too great and the contents could not be pumped out, but would come back in! After that depth it was buckets . . .

"Later in the War we developed what were called 'high-pressure heads.' These could be safely used at greater depths, though mishandling

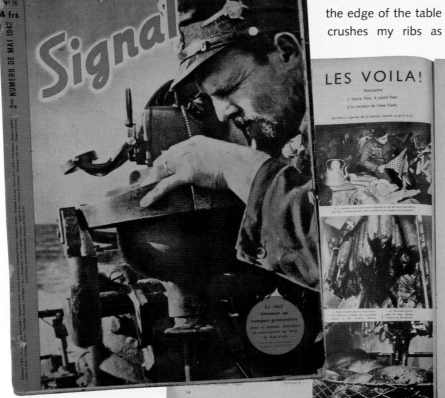

Above right: The forward head (toilet) aboard U995, which was situated immediately aft of the bow room. Mishandling of the pumping system could result in disaster, as was the sorry case for U1206.

Left: The French-language Signal magazine dedicated a lot of space to a report of a patrol aboard U96. The correspondent responsible for this article was actually Lothar-Günther Buchheim, whose experience on patrol was later fictionalized in the book and movie, Das Boot.

them could spell disaster. It was a very complex device and men were actually specially trained to use them, gaining a certificate from the rest of the crew and the salubrious title of 'Toilet Expert.' It was all very amusing, but not so for one boat that left Norway in the final weeks of the War. The new combat boat, *U1206*, was actually lost through mishandling the system. Apparently the captain, *Kptlt* Karl-Adolf Schlitt, attempted to use the device and was assisted by an appointed expert despatched by the boat's LI. [In different versions of this story, the captain was in the engine room and so was not himself responsible for these events.] Between them they managed to follow the correct procedure and received not only the toilet contents all over them, but also a thick, uncontrollable stream of water. The boat began to flood and the LI attempted to take it up to relieve the outside pressure. However, water entered the batteries and produced chlorine gas, which is deadly. The bilge pump failed, and next minute the boat was on the surface and came under aircraft attack. The boat was out of control and Schlitt ordered everybody out, the boat abandoned and scuttled. Three men were actually killed and the rest captured—all because of the head."

U-boat crockery

Somewhat surprisingly, given the limited space available, proper porcelain crockery was carried for the crew to use at mealtimes. When not being used, it was stored in lockers in the compartments in which the crew ate their meals. Shallow bowls and small mugs were provided for all the crew, while a slightly more varied array of serving bowls and platters was available for use in the Officers' Mess.

Several manufacturers supplied the *Kriegsmarine* and its U-boat service— KPM Royal of Berlin, Koenigszelt of Silesia, Bauscher Weiden (the first German specialist manufacturers of hotel porcelain), Jaeger & Company of Marktredwitz, and Hutschenreuther of Hohenberg, Bavaria, all provided crockery. Most items manufactured for the *Kriegsmarine* were stamped on the reverse with the Nazi eagle and swastika, above a large capital 'M,' which designated it for Marine use.

Cutlery produced for the *Kriegsmarine* was marked in the same way. Each crewman tended to keep his own knife, fork, and spoon among his personal belongings when at sea. Indeed, the wreck of *U869*, which was discovered off the New Jersey coast in 1991, was eventually identified by means of a wooden-handled knife recovered from the site—for on it, the boat's radio operator, Martin Horenburg, had inscribed his name.

Above: *The crest of the KPM Royal porcelain manufacturer of Berlin, surmounted by the eagle, swastika, and "M," denoting naval issue.*

Above: *Such manufacturer markings were on the underside of each piece of issue porcelain, but they were never accompanied by individual boat numbers.*

Wireless Station, Listening Room, and Captain's Quarters

"Toward the end the order to submerge didn't come from the commander anymore but from the radio operator."—Herbert Guschewski, *U869*

Immediately forward of the control room, and separated from it by a heavy watertight door, were the U-boat's "listening" and radio rooms—the effective eyes and ears of a U-boat. Correspondingly, directly opposite these two vital compartments was the captain's "cabin," which in effect consisted of his bunk, a small writing desk, a seat, and his personal cupboard. Able to be screened off from the narrow corridor that ran the boat's length by a heavy, green felt curtain, this "cabin" constituted the sole "private" space on board the entire boat. A compass repeater situated above his cupboard allowed the captain to check the boat's course as he lay within earshot of the radio room, hydrophone, and control room.

Men often chose the option to train as a telegraphist in preference over "unskilled" seaman duties. However, to qualify as a radio operator (*Funker*) the candidate's aptitude would first be determined by various intelligence, psychological, and hearing tests. If the candidate passed these he was allowed to commence training, which began with three months of basic military drill on the island of Dänholm at Stralsund in northern Germany. This was then followed by six months at Flensburg's naval radio school, learning basic telegraphy skills. If his psychological profile had indicated a capacity for "small unit work" the candidate could be transferred compulsorily to the U-boat service, though many volunteered for what was perceived to be the most illustrious branch of the *Kriegsmarine*.

Left: The small radio room aboard U995. A range of frequencies was covered by various transmitters and receivers, which were manned by a rotating shift of telegraphers.

Posting to the general U-boat crew training division at Gotenhafen followed on from further training at Flensburg on U-boat telegraphy techniques. Finally, special courses for hydrophone work and the operation of radar and radar-detection devices would be given; knowledge of the latter was updated between patrols as various new models of detector emerged in the escalating electronics war between 1939 and 1945.

The BdU used frequent radio transmissions to organize U-boat patrol lines: two rotating shifts of four men—one non-commissioned officer and one ordinary seaman on each shift—manned the stations under the overall supervision of the boat's IIWO. Aboard a combat U-boat, standard German time was observed no matter where the boat was located, in order to maintain consistency in the working environment. The daytime hours between 08:00 and 20:00 were divided into three four-hour watches, the remaining 12 night hours, with their decreased signal traffic, into two six-hour watches. Thus the duty time of each man was rotated daily while maintaining an overall 12 hours on station.

Standard duties for the signals crew included sending and receiving radio messages, operating the Enigma encryption machine, hydrophone use when submerged, operation of whatever radar and radar detection devices were installed, and acting as the boat's medical officer if no doctor was on board (a flexible state of affairs throughout the War). The chief telegraphist's final task would be to type up the captain's handwritten War Diary notes. (In some boats the commander dictated notes for the diary.) This moment-by-moment account of the patrol would later be scrutinized, analyzed, and explained by the captain in a personal meeting either with Dönitz himself or with senior officers of the U-boat Command before being filed in U-boat Command's permanent records. (Six copies were made of each report.)

The listening room housed the boat's hydrophone receiver, which enabled the U-boat to "hear" what was going on around it, detecting individual ships at up to 12 miles (20km), a convoy at 62 miles (100km). Later in the War the basic system comprised a passive sonar device: a receiver connected to two semi-circular arrays of small

Opposite page, clockwise from left: A Lorenz-manufactured transmitter-receiver; the hydrophone, or listening, room aboard U995. Receivers for radars were here, as well as radar detectors and, of course, the all-important hydrophone gear; receiver for the Wanze radar detector; radio tube testing equipment; the hydrophone display panel.

diaphragms positioned forward of the bow dive planes. An electronic timer linked to each diaphragm measured which one received a sound pulse first, providing a rudimentary directional bearing to the source.

Aft of the listening room was the radio room, with its various radio transmitters and receivers, cipher equipment, and any radar or radar detection devices. The number and make of radio sets aboard individual U-boats differed somewhat, though they all carried enough radios to cover the three main wavelengths: Short Wave, Medium Wave, and Long or Very Long Wave. Short Wave communication allowed U-boats to communicate with BdU. With this, broadcasts were facilitated by means of jumper wires that trailed fore and aft of the conning tower; a telescopic rod antenna mounted on the conning tower later augmented this somewhat rough and ready system.

Medium Wave (MW) communications allowed U-boats at sea to coordinate with each other. When used in conjunction with the direction-finding loop mounted on the conning tower, MW was used primarily to transmit and receive the beacon signals that were employed to form a "Wolf Pack." MW was also used to monitor general enemy surface-ship communication and radio broadcasts. The receiver could be linked to the boat's loudspeaker system so that the crew could hear the latest news and music from Germany, too. The radio room crew was also in charge of the gramophone that was normally carried on board, though it was not standard issue.

Long and Very Long Wavebands were used to receive messages while submerged at periscope depth—these proved essential in the later stages of the War, when U-boats were forced to spend longer periods submerged simply to survive.

If fitted, radar—never perfected on World War II U-boats—was operated from the radio room, as were the myriad detectors that tracked enemy beams. These emitted frequent audible pulses—the closer the enemy drew, the louder the sound of the pulse became. As it was the operator of these detectors who was the first to be aware of an imminent enemy aircraft attack, it was he who largely advised when an emergency dive was required. The escalating electronics war necessitated frequent changes to the installations used aboard the U-boats, as well as sporadic training to update the communications crew, either in Germany, or locally to the U-boat bases.

Sending and receiving messages

While the captain was ultimately responsible for the duration of messages, the ability of the Allies to locate U-boats by their radio direction meant the longer a U-boat was "pinned" to the surface transmitting and receiving messages, the more likely it was to be found. Dönitz did not hesitate to admonish captains he considered to have made frivolous transmissions.

The first attacks (1)

Naval service offered many men the chance to learn a technical trade. Georg Högel of *U30* and *U110* remembers how he came to serve on U-boats—and about his involvement in the very first U-boat attack of World War II:

"I was always interested in U-boats before I came to the military. I was a typographer—I worked in a printing press and had done so for four years. My boss had been a navy man during the war [the Boxer Rebellion] in China. Since then he had been in the navy *Kameradschaft* and when they had anything to print he was given it and he printed it for nothing! So, in the end I was given it to print and I read one leaflet that said: 'We need men for the navy.' I looked and saw that the courses would take just two years instead of the four and a half years for the *Luftwaffe*. So, I thought, things happen much more quickly in the navy and at my age four and a half years was too long. I looked at courses in telegraphy in the navy and joined at Christmas.

"First, I was at school for telegraphy and then I had half a year of infantry training, followed by another half year at Flensburg for more

Above: *The passenger liner SS* Athenia *going down. The attack was a propaganda disaster for the* Kriegsmarine *as it evoked memories of the sinking of the* Lusitania *in 1915.*

telegraphy, and then they said, where would you like to go—battleships, destroyers, cruisers? And I said only to U-boats. But there was a part of me that thought, this is crazy, the U-boat service won't take me as I was only signed on for two years, but they did. I was the only one—the other three men taken aboard the U-boats for telegraphy were all officers. I was the only ordinary seaman."

[Högel was soon posted:] "*U30* was my first boat, which I joined in 1937 when I was 18 years old. We went to Spain after the Civil War had ended. I took part in lots of exercises in peacetime, and it was a very interesting part of my life. But I must say that you could feel in the last year before war that the situation was getting slowly worse and that war was definitely coming. We had no Saturday, Sunday or free time; we were exercising all the time—training always. But we were young and in a way it was exciting. When the War started I was 20."

[On the day War was declared between Britain and Germany—September 3, 1939—*U30* launched its maiden attack.] "My Captain [Fritz-Julius] Lemp saw the *Athenia* at 16:30 hours as the ship was crossing our path. We followed it, waiting for darkness. Then we went nearer, so that Lemp could take a good look at the *Athenia*. He felt that she had hidden guns. He thought it was not a civilian ship as it was darkened at night and zig-zagging, and believed that it was a Q-ship—

Below left: *First-generation Type VII U-boats of the Saltzwedel Flotilla in Wilhelms-haven. The numbers, removed in September 1939, date this photo to before the War.*
Below right: *Kptlt Fritz Julius Lemp in Wilhelmshaven. Though a skilled captain, his name would forever be associated with the* Athenia *and* Enigma *episodes.*

Above, left and right: Standard-issue U-boat radio headphones manufactured by Telefunken. (Right) Oberfunkmaat *Rudi Elkerhausen at work transmitting messages from U564. Elkerhausen was killed aboard this boat when it was sunk by British aircraft in the Bay of Biscay on June 14, 1943—none of the boat's technical crew survived the sinking.*

a warship disguised as a merchant used to trap U-boats that tried attacking on the surface. So we torpedoed it.

"We shot three torpedoes, but one of them hung up in the tube and exploded on the surface after we managed to free it. But the *Athenia* was hit anyway and began to sink. We never surfaced until after we had shot, and then we stayed on the dark side of the ship, with the moon before us. I heard the radio transmissions but we saw we couldn't do anything as we realized there were so many people onboard." [To his dread Lemp was informed by Högel of the ship's true identity as the young radioman translated the intercepted transmission from the stricken *Athenia*. She was not, in fact, a "Q" ship but a transatlantic passenger liner carrying 1,103 civilians, including 300 Americans. The attack on the *Athenia* was a propaganda disaster for the Germans, reviving as it did memories of the sinking by U-boats of the passenger liner *Lusitania* in 1915. The attack on the *Athenia* was officially denied and all references to it were later removed from *U30*'s War Diary by Högel, on Dönitz's orders.]

"The *Athenia* was dreadful. We were one little boat and we would have been unable to rescue 1,200 people. It was a very difficult situation, especially for Lemp. He was a good commander . . . and the next time Lemp was firing torpedoes against England he was also a correct commander when we sunk the *Blairlogie*. He behaved impeccably. I must

also tell you with the *Blairlogie* I was very impressed with the radioman—he was sending to the last.

"Days later, on September 14, I and my comrades from *U30* had our nerves severely tested and I was put into an embarrassing situation. Even now, years and years later, I can't forget this day. It is entrenched in my memory like notches cut into tree bark. We found a ship in the North Channel—the SS *Fanad Head*. We were traveling in a light wind and scattered cloud west of Northern Ireland. From the east we saw a steamer. She was traveling in strong zig-zags so we set course to intercept. When it saw us it immediately turned on a reciprocal heading and began transmitting an SOS that I could hear over the radio. We were hunting at full speed and had little difficulty in overhauling the ship, which ignored our semaphore order to stop and shots from our 88mm across the bow. Eventually we fired on it and it stopped while the captain and crew abandoned ship. So far, so good. It was the first steamer that we had a chance to go aboard, the two others had been sunk. You see, we had a slight menu problem aboard *U30*: we had no bread!

The first attacks (2)

"A telegram had fetched me back prematurely from vacation for this patrol with war looming. In Hannover I saw our *Maschinenmaat*, Adolf Schmidt, who would also normally have returned from vacation in the homeland. But, apparently in order not to have to make him return prematurely, another leading seaman took over his task. You see, on a U-boat every service grade had a second task to fulfil and he was our NCO responsible for provisions. However, when we were at sea and the supply of fresh bread that we had taken with us at the beginning of the journey—which had spent ten to 14 days being carried in hammocks—had shrunk to a few moldy and inedible remains, it meant that we were on to canned bread. So . . . no sooner said than done. But when the first box was opened it was full of cans of milk. Hello, what's this? The next box, the same, and another. *Verdammt!* Where the hell is the bread? Also, the whole periscope well was packed with canned bread, only it wasn't. It was damned milk! All boxes full of milk. What a mistake to make! Twelve days at sea and no more bread, with another four to six weeks of patrolling ahead.

"Milk with rice, milk with raisins, milk with dry potatoes, milk with eggs, I couldn't take anymore of these home-made specialties and was really developing an aversion to milk! . . . But now we had a new hope with the SS *Fanad Head* after the crew had abandoned her. So that we could save torpedoes we were going to board the ship and destroy it with explosives—after going through her galley!

"Myself, I had not seen her. My place was in the radio room, and there I had been on a 12-hour watch. Naturally I understood why the steamer was signaling as soon as we had begun our attack, the ether alive with the message 'SSS. Chased by German submarine!' As quickly as possible I, with my Morse key on the same wavelength, sent 'Stay off your key,' as one called in such circumstances until the transmissions stopped. We did this for two reasons: first, to keep them from calling help to the scene and second, so that we wouldn't have to open fire on them to silence the radio. Finally, they stopped and their crew left in small boats. But it had been too late. Our

boarding crew made it to the ship, searched her for bread, but aircraft from the [British aircraft carrier] *Ark Royal*, which was nearby, arrived and attacked, injuring one man. But they actually managed to also bring themselves down! Flying too low, they were damaged by their own bomb explosions while we disappeared below the surface in a hurry. In the end we retrieved our men, some food, and an English guest—the pilot, Guy Griffiths—who we fished out of the water."

Top left: Hand-made cover for the radio log in which every outgoing radio message was recorded aboard U446; it was donated to the U-boat Archive by Dr Hans Weidemann, who served aboard the boat as IIWO. Commissioned into the Kriegsmarine on June 20, 1942, U446 never saw action—it struck a British aerial mine three months and a day later, and sank with the loss of 23 men—including the commander—aboard.

Below left: Pancakes at sea. Rations were carefully planned, so the discovery that bread had not been loaded aboard U30 at the dockside caused a major headache for the crew.

Below right: These two officers in their mess appear less than impressed with the fare on offer. An army is said to march on its stomach . . . but food is as crucial to the navy.

Radio op—and medic

As the course of the War progressed, many U-boats, particularly the larger Type IXs and *Milchkuh* Type XIV supply U-boats, but also including several Type VIIs, carried medical personnel as a matter of course. However, before then it was the duty of the chief radio operator to act as medical orderly. Georg Seitz remembered:

"As radioman I was the medic aboard *U604* and in charge of the medical supplies and treating whatever problems we had. I'm sure it was because as radiomen we had nimble—and clean—hands. *Kptlt* Höltring often insisted that he had access to the medical cabinet to use the scalpel for carving small models while he was aboard, so that was another reason for disagreements because I would say, 'That is for wounded men, not for playing with.' But he would insist—and he was the captain.

"We would attend short courses at Carnac near Lorient [in France] to learn and relearn basic first aid—everything from toothache to gonorrhea!

Sometimes we had no problems but other times we had lots of things to deal with, but I have to say I was happier when on *U873* it was the medical officer's— Walter Ortwein's—job!"

Above and below: Fascinatingly intimate photographs of Kptlt Horst Höltring building a model sailing ship aboard U604—using the boat's medical scalpels to make it . . .

An enemy aboard

Lieutenant Guy Griffiths was in fact a Royal Marines pilot, the first to be captured in World War II. He and the second pilot, Lieutenant Thursden, were rescued by *U30*, but their air gunners were killed in the action. Griffiths was able to witness the workings of *U30* first hand, forming a close bond with Georg Högel. This text is from a letter written to Högel by Griffiths:

"I have never forgotten the care and attention all the crew of *U30* gave to the wounded Lieutenant Thursden, [who was] so badly burnt. As the crew ran past his bunk to go to Action Stations, at Lemp's instructions, the last man past would tuck in the blanket, which had been pulled out by the passing seamen, before moving to his post. I also remember your Chief Engineer, the black-bearded Eichelborn who, after you had landed your wounded seaman by dinghy off Iceland, came down into the control center with a large turkey that he named the '*Deutsche Adler*' [German eagle]. What with our Skua attacks, the subsequent attacks by Swordfish aircraft and later—after circling the area of the *Fanad Head*—being depth charged by the *Ark Royal* escort destroyers, it was all too exciting for a pilot who preferred to be up in the air and not under the sea.

"I seem to recall not being allowed to linger by the radio room, and also remember being allowed up to the bridge to get fresh air at night. A day or two after I came aboard one of your crew, who did not look as if he liked us very much, showed me a piece of bomb shrapnel (from our attack) that had been taken out of his ear!

"The last morning, September 28, when *U30* was tied up alongside the dock and Lemp and the officers got out the Schnapps for a farewell drink, I remember the escort arriving to take us off, stopping us from that drink. Thursden was escorted to the naval hospital, while I was put into a Horch open car with the escorts all pointing pistols at me! As you may know, Thursden and I had become 'political prisoners' and did not exist officially. Hitler was claiming that Churchill had staged the sinking of the *Athenia* to involve the US against Germany, claiming no U-boat was in the area. When Lemp signaled that he had picked us up he was in trouble, for the whole affair became a political matter. It was not until December 1939 that, through another PoW, I was able to get a message to my fiancée that I was still alive."

Above, left to right: *The sinking of U604, damaged by US bombers. The crew abandoned ship and swam to the U-boats summoned to assist. Half of the survivors were eventually helped aboard U172 (foreground) and U185. Höltring—seen saluting in Brest during happier days in November 1942 (far right photo)—did not survive; he shot himself after U185 was also subsequently attacked and sunk.*
Left: *Guy Griffiths, photographed as a PoW In Germany. After making several abortive escape attempts, he finally succeeded in 1945.*

The radiomen manning the hydrophones were often the first to locate enemy shipping, and thus had to direct their captains during submerged combat. They also had to be careful not give their boat's position away to the enemy through over-free use of the radio. The responsibility could sometimes be an onerous burden, as Georg Seitz of *U604* described:

"My boat was part of the 9th U-Flotilla at Brest [in France]. The flotilla was formed while we sailed out from Germany. Our captain, Höltring, had a worrying habit of writing long messages, which I had to transmit. I used to tell him, 'The enemy will DF [Direction Find] us with such a long message,' but I sent them anyway. And so Höltring and I, we had some conflict. But we were still a successful boat. When in *U604* I was the radioman who transmitted the beacon signals for other U-boats of the

Knappen Group onto convoy ON166 as we shadowed the convoy. The battle was massive—14 merchants sunk with what we thought were two U-boats missing. [In fact, four U-boats were sunk in total during the battle.] But we had a near thing. During the night we followed the convoy slowly, sending our signal every half hour to bring other boats. We had been told by Dönitz not to attack but to gather and attack all together. We had radar, but the men on the bridge watched through the night as we skirted the ships. But they found us. An American destroyer [Coast Guard Cutter USS *Spencer*] charged and we went under. The captain ordered an emergency dive and we began to play mouse to this hungry cat.

"I could hear the American. The slow thump of merchant ship propellers was different to the higher sound of the warships. Every time we turned and tried to get him off us, his screws would turn faster and he would pass overhead. The earphones let me listen to him until the splashes were heard. Then it was time to take the earphones off and hold on. But it

was not like in the movies: there was no shouting, there was no noise. The depth charges knocked us around and even threw men to the floor, but we stayed quiet. If we could hear him . . . he could hear us! Then the noise of the ship would go quiet . . . he was listening. So we crept this way and then that, but he followed, his sonar bouncing on our boat. More propellers, more depth charges, some leaks, and even a small problem with the diesel. Höltring held his calm. We survived and the American went away. Now it was our turn, and we later torpedoed a ship— the one with their direction-finding mast on top so that the other boats were now harder for the Americans to find.

"After the patrol I accompanied Höltring to see Dönitz, he with the boat's War Diary and myself with the radio log, to explain things to the Admiral. I came away from the meeting with a signed photograph of Dönitz."

Left: Funkmaat *Georg Seitz on the foredeck of U604 on returning to Brest. When U604 was sunk on August 11, 1943, Seitz survived. He later served aboard the large Type IXD2, U873.*

Enigma and the intelligence war

"Every key stroke produced a different letter, with millions of combinations. How could it be broken?"—Hans-Rudolf Rösing

Key to the transmission of messages between U-boat command and the boats fighting at sea was a secure code system. In 1939, Germany possessed one of the most sophisticated cipher machines in existence: the Enigma. This had begun life as a commercial tool for transmitting company secrets in Berlin during 1923 before the German military adopted and adapted it for use, the later *Kriegsmarine* version of which was known as *Schlüsselmaschine M* ("Code writer M"—for Marine). It was a "passive" coding machine, in that it did not transmit, but merely enciphered and deciphered, relying on a standard Morse signal to carry the coded message. It comprised an input keyboard, light board to display the enciphered letter, plug board of 26 double sockets, and rotor system of either three or four rotors in use from a possible selection of between five and eight. Each time a key was depressed an electric pulse traveled a complex, constantly rotating path through the plugboard and each rotor before illuminating the coded equivalent letter. With a dizzying number of variable rotor and plugboard settings the net result was a staggering 129,651,786,900,000,000,000,000 variable code combinations. Once a message was coded, a radio operator then transmitted it in seemingly meaningless five-letter groups. However, two operators at either end of the Enigma communication, with the same plugboard settings and rotor choice and starting position, could replicate the message, simply inputting the enciphered letters to produce plain text.

While Allied code-breakers managed to crack the *Luftwaffe* and *Wehrmacht* Enigma ciphers during the War's early stages, the more complex *Kriegsmarine* system defied all attempts at penetration. The Allies' first break came with the capture of an intact codebook and rotors from the German weather-reporting ship *München*, which was boarded by men from the British destroyer HMS *Somali* on May 7, 1941. However, while this enabled the team at Bletchley Park in England to

Below: *To achieve the tight control that allowed U-boats to rendezvous at sea, Dönitz relied on frequent messages, transmitted once encoded on Enigma. Later, after the German ciphers were broken, such reliance would become the U-boats' Achilles' heel.*

Left: *A U-boat Enigma machine. Concerned that his codes might have been compromised, Dönitz introduced a fourth rotor to the machines his service used. This cipher of increased complexity caused an intelligence "blackout" in Britain, which lasted for most of 1942 until this code, too, was broken. Penetration of the Enigma—used by all of Germany's armed forces—contributed to the defeat of Nazi Germany on all fronts.*

Right: Funkmaat *Willi Anderheyden uses the four-rotor Enigma machine in the radio room aboard U564. The pad on which he is writing the encoded message appears to be resting on the turntable of the U-boat's gramophone.*

crack the low-grade weather code, it still did not enable them to decode the far more complicated system used by combat units, such as destroyers and U-boats. In May 1941 the capture of codebooks and an intact Enigma machine from *U110* finally allowed the breaking of the U-boat's "Triton" code. But February 1942 saw the introduction of the fourth rotor to the U-boat machines—it was not until October 1942 when men from HMS *Petard* were able to board the sinking *U559* in the Mediterranean and capture more codebooks, that this new system, named "Shark" in Britain, was also cracked. Two of the boarding party, Francis Anthony Blair Fasson and Able Seaman Colin Grazier, were unable to escape the sinking U-boat and were killed. Both were posthumously awarded the George Cross, though their real achievement would not be publicly known for 30 more years, as the Allied code-breaking achievement—named ULTRA as a reflection of its importance—remained a closely guarded secret. The Type IX *U505* also yielded an intact Enigma machine when the US Navy captured the boat on June 4, 1944.

The breaking of the Enigma code, and the Germans' reliance on it for Dönitz's closely controlled U-boat dispositions, ultimately proved to be the U-boats' Achilles' heel. Perhaps never before has an opponent been so fully informed of his enemy's movements and intentions as the Allies had been during World War II.

Some daily duties

Privy as they were to restricted information, radio operators had to be careful what they told their fellow crewmembers. Some, meanwhile, used their position to help raise the morale of men aboard their boat, as *Funkmaat* **Joachim Gürke of** *U995* **remembered:**

"I knew everything, almost as much as the captain. I knew the orders from U-boat Command, the weather forecast, reports from other boats . . . Men in the NCO wardroom would ask, 'Is there anything new, Joachim?' I tried to keep my cards on the table because I knew the feeling that only a rumor like 'destroyer nearby' made the pulse race . . . my single principle was to keep the excitement under control, within the limits of my obligation to keep certain messages secret. Sometimes I motivated them to wake up with the words: 'We are expecting a convoy tomorrow.'

"But we didn't think of classes, we didn't live in this big metal tube in a strictly divided hierarchy. I always tried to see things from the officers' perspective. There was one long depth-charge hunt by several English destroyers. From my hydrophone, I glanced at the captain. In a grim terse way he gave his orders to try and shake off the pursuit. My first feeling was not one of sympathy: he has brought us into this fatal situation, this idiot . . . After some 50 depth charges and ear-deafening noises of screws in my ears I had changed my mind about this man: my goodness, he is alone, the only one of the crew whose orders decided life and death for all of us. And suddenly I became quiet. After all, he was with us—why bother? So we suffered and we found support in each other, without regard to ranks."

The captain of *U995*, **Hans-Georg Hess, talked about the vital role played by the hydrophone operator:**

"Underwater we were dependent on the sharp ears of the hydrophone operator in the listening room. Far east of Murmansk on December 26, 1944, the sound man reported a Russian guard ship detected by hydrophone at a distance of about 64km [40 miles]. He heard the noises of the pistons. *U995* emerged and laid course to 120° in the direction of the sound. After 30 minutes an armed trawler came into view and after another half an hour it was sunk by artillery [that is, by *U995*'s heavy Flak weaponry]. We rescued a 17-year-old Russian—the second prisoner on this cruise during the end of 1944. For this *Funkgast* Alfred Ottine got the Iron Cross First Class."

Although the radio and hydrophone operators may have been aware of their boat's orders, they were not responsible for navigation and were therefore as ignorant as most of the crew about their actual position. *Funkobergefreiter* **Herbert Selinger recalled one interesting incident:**

"The story of the German commander who didn't know whether he was in Brest or not, and suddenly discovered he was outside Portsmouth

Above: *The slightly larger radio room on a Type IX U-boat. All radio traffic was monitored; relevant transmissions—both friendly and enemy—were then passed on to the captain for operational use.*

instead . . . Well, that was us in *U763*! We left Brest on June 20, 1944, and on July 5 were situated in the English Channel. After an attack on a convoy we were pinned and hunted by depth-charge attack for 36 hours. We had no way of fixing our position and crept at slow speed—unknowingly—in the direction of Portsmouth. After the attack had ended and there were no more screw noises in the hydrophones we surfaced and began heading toward the harbor. Now, for the first time, we realized something wasn't right. We did a sharp about turn, dived, and found a hole while studying the map. We were able to take a depth sounding that showed us we were in Spithead, right outside Portsmouth. We slowly crept out in the shadow of a convoy, then headed straight for France as soon as we were able to move into free water. That's a true story!"

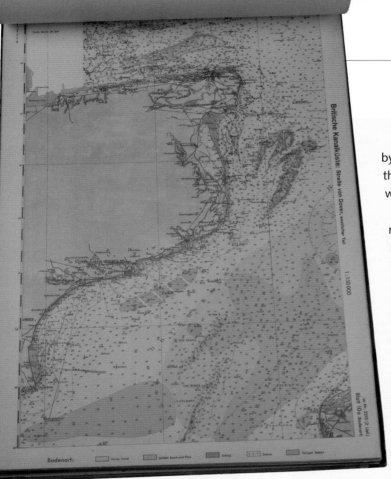

Also during 1944, *U953* was part of the group of U-boats sent to counter the overwhelming strength of the Allied invasion armada off the Normandy coast. Her skipper, Karl-Heinz Marbach, had already clashed with his superiors over dubious attack orders that seemed to demand the impossible. At sea, things did not improve. "When we set off for patrol, invasion fever was at its height. At any rate, I was not a little surprised when, soon after leaving base, the IIWO—who was also wireless officer—told me that he had clean forgotten the codeword for setting the cipher key. That meant we could neither encipher nor decipher W/T messages [neither transmit nor receive].

"We couldn't return to base—in those days it would have looked too much like cowardice—and, in any case, after my private row with the Flag Officer of U-boats (FdU West), it was unthinkable. So, the IIWO tried to elicit the codeword from a passing U-boat: too strange a request altogether! They never deigned to reply.

"For the whole of one night and the following day, he tried to get the answer

by process of elimination, testing no less than 6,000 of the more likely words to see if they would fit. While this was going on we lay off Brest, cruising slowly in a circle.

"The following night (the word must have been number 6,001), we determined to put out a W/T call by the 'Hand Emergency Method' in plain language. Ten times we tried, and got no answer, the ether never even shuddered. During the process, so as to show as little of the boat as possible, we surfaced at an angle with only the forward section of the jumper wire with attached aerial and part of the superstructure above water.

"The next night, getting desperate, we made five six-minute calls—transmitting for 1,800 seconds through air thick with enemy aircraft, using the same method and telling the world of our misfortunes. It was incredible but even that bought no result. Half an hour later, when we were underwater again, the W/T operator suddenly announced that he had been transmitting on the wrong frequency! So we tried once more, for another 15 minutes, and at last that time got an answer. It was none too soon, for a few minutes later our position was floodlit by parachute flares dropped by aircraft. But by then we were no longer to be seen.

"There was no disciplinary action: what would the point have been in charging a man with, (i) youth, (ii) inexperience, (iii) having the invasion jitters? After our return from the patrol the wireless officer confessed to me why he had forgotten the codeword. The morning we sailed, he had learnt that his father had been arrested by the Gestapo and sent to a concentration camp."

Far left: *A Kriegsmarine* atlas; *this page covers the English Channel. The map showed depth and seabed conditions.*

Below: *Coded radio traffic criss-crossed all seas in which U-boats operated.*

Below: *Radio equipment at FdU West HQ in Angers, France; this—with the huge transmitter in Germany—made control of Wolf Packs possible.*

The captain's role

The relationship between U-boat men was close, but the captain was ultimately responsible for the safety of the crew, and how he acted affected the atmosphere on the entire boat. Erich Topp, one of the *Kriegsmarine*'s U-boat "Aces," remembered this clearly:

"The most important characteristic for a U-boat commander in my opinion was that you have a sense of responsibility for all of the men onboard and that you have to know the personal situation and strengths and weaknesses of everybody. Because everybody has to know what they have to do, and you have to know what they are capable of. Strong comradeship. Two of my old boat crews [*U57* and *U552*] still meet every year because those years were such an important part of our lives. Living and working so closely with these men I couldn't compare with any other situation in life. It leaves a special bond.

"The Type VII had the same diving time as my old boat, the Type II. But the Type II *U57* was much smaller, of course. I had no space to myself. I slept in the bow room with the torpedoes and the rest of the crew, and had no privileges. I would be woken alongside everybody else when men were moving about. Before my first command I had been the Watch Officer aboard *U46* and made four patrols. But my commanding officer was not really very good. He did not attack and I think his main goal was to survive. So, when I took over *U57*, I said to myself, 'You must change that.' So, I decided to be aggressive in my approach. For example, on one patrol to the west of Ireland we were attacked by a bomber and were heavily damaged. It was a very bad attack from my

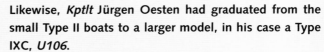

Above: *The* U-boat Commander's Handbook, *containing advice compiled by the German Naval Command; it was distributed to all active service commanders.*

point of view and the boat was left in a bad state. Anyhow, as a consequence one diesel was knocked off its foundation so I only had one diesel remaining. So, I called a meeting of my Watch Officer and the Chief Engineer, who said, 'Of course, with only one diesel we have to go home to repair. If the other diesel breaks down we are lost!' But that was neither my opinion nor that of my Watch Officer. We still had all of our torpedoes on board! So I said, 'We now have only a lower speed so we have to go into the Lion's jaws,' so we went in close to Liverpool past the channel lights. A convoy came out and we attacked with three torpedoes . . . we got three hits and then of course were chased by destroyers. We had to dive and we had only 50m [164ft] of water beneath us. We sat there for 36 hours and everything was breaking down under depth charge attacks. The crew looked to me to reassure them: we were all in it together. Fortunately we survived and the following night we tried to surface. But the boat had so much water inside that we couldn't move. One electric motor was still operating and I kept using it until we pulled free and rose. We survived. I must say, I had overdone it a little that time, but I learned. Nevertheless, we reloaded the tubes with the last two reserve torpedoes and we attacked another convoy, but we had 100m [328ft] beneath us that time. We sank a tanker and escaped. But it was a great experience and lesson to me: not to overdo it."

Likewise, *Kptlt* Jürgen Oesten had graduated from the small Type II boats to a larger model, in his case a Type IXC, *U106*.

"During my time as commander of the small *U61* I had some trouble in the North Sea. I attacked a convoy and in turn was attacked by enemy destroyers. I was forced to bottom the boat at 134m [440ft] while they pounded us for hours with depth charges. One blast was so severe that

Above: *A U-boat commander prepares himself in his tiny "cabin." Separated from the corridor by a green curtain, it was the only semi-private space aboard a Type VIIC.*

it actually dented the pressure hull and knocked a diesel off its foundation. We were lucky the hull did not collapse. We had no lights and the destroyers must have thought that they had had a kill because they left, leaving only a trawler on the site to make sure we did not reappear. Hours later we managed to get the boat on top, but we only had emergency lights. One of these lights was at the base of the conning tower, but because they were emergency lights running on DC current you couldn't switch it off. I got up into the tower, saw the trawler, and then also saw that bloody light shining up at me! I raced down, got my fist, and smashed the thing to put it out. Well, we managed to get clear and nursed the boat back to Wilhelmshaven, where Dönitz and his staff were waiting at the lock. He said to me, 'Well, you're not supposed to be here. You're supposed to be

Right: This crude-looking device calculated the deflection required to shoot the torpedoes. Aligning the various dials in a combination that took in the U-boat's and target's course, plus periscope orientation, the setting for a shot could be calculated.

Left: The captain's "cabin" on U995, offset to port of the central passageway, opposite the radio and listening rooms.
Right: Kptlt Heinz von Davidson, U281's commander. The seahorse emblem is from his earlier Bordfliegerstaffel (Shipboard Squadron) 1/196.

dead.' I replied, 'Yes, Sir, but if you don't like it, I can always go back!' Days later my crew gathered some fragments of the light and mounted it on a board with a picture of a fist next to it. That's how we had got away.

"Later, when I moved to *U106*, well, I had my own area within the boat with a bunk, desk, and even a small foldaway washbasin! Luxury! But the problems of leading the boat, the responsibilities were the same, no matter what size she was."

Control Room and Bridge

"I was always seasick for the first few days at sea, but medicine helped, as did fresh air. I was never sick on the bridge."—Hans-Rudolf Rösing, *U48*

Centrally located within the U-boat's pressure hull was the control room, aptly named the *zentrale* by German crews. Within this compartment lay the nerve-center of the boat's operational systems. The diving and trim controls, main helm position, navigator's station, and navigation periscope were all situated here, as were myriad other systems such as the bilge pump, periscope motor, and fresh-water purifier (which was used to produce fresh water from salt water).

The large periscope found within the *zentrale* was for navigation purposes; this was also used to search the sky for enemy aircraft before the boat surfaced. Although commonly seen in propaganda photographs and movies as the station used by the captain for submerged firing, the navigation periscope was in fact rarely used in attacks as it did not possess the necessary range markings, unlike the attack periscope. The 25ft (7.5m) long navigation scope was a hand-trained, high-angle device that possessed a thicker shaft and larger head than the attack version. This allowed greater light entry and thus superior vision, but it also created a larger wake and so was more visible on the surface.

Both the chief engineer and navigator were often to be found on duty within the control room. When in the control room (and whether the boat was at action stations or not), the chief engineer would sit behind the two planesmen who controlled the boat's hydroplanes. One planesman operated the bow planes, the other those at

Left: Hydroplane controls on U995, manufactured by Swiss-based Brown, Boveri, and Co. The planes were moved using the push-buttons; the outer wheels were for emergency use only.

the stern. Although they sat facing two large handwheels, these were used only in emergencies: the hydroplanes were in fact operated by two simple push-buttons. Two depth-gauges assisted the planesmen. One, finely graduated to a depth of 82ft (25m), was used during periscope observation while the second, less accurate, gauge was used at greater depths.

Immediately to the planesmen's left was the helm. This was operated at important moments, for example when the boat was at action stations, by a seaman who was assigned the duty of senior helmsman for the duration of the mission. Again, the helm was operated by means of two push-buttons.

The helmsman had three different stations to man. The first—the main steering position—was within the *zentrale* itself; this was used when the boat was submerged. A second station, in the conning tower, was reached via a ladder from the *zentrale*; this was used during surface engagements. Here, as in the *zentrale*, the helmsman would take his orders from the captain, who would be on the bridge during this time. The final steering position was on the bridge itself, and this was used purely when at maneuvering stations—when docking, or leaving port.

Alongside the auxiliary helm in the limited space of the conning tower were the torpedo calculator and attack periscope. During submerged torpedo attacks, the captain sat on the periscope's narrow saddle, rotating the scope by means of foot pedals. Meanwhile, he controlled the periscope's height using a hand-operated lever. With his other hand (usually his right hand, if the captain was right-handed) and using another lever, he adjusted the upper prism in the head of the scope to change his field of view. This ranged between 15° below the horizon to 20° above it.

Continuing up the ladder that stretched from the *zentrale* below was the bridge, which was reached via the conning-tower hatch. At sea this was the only hatch in general use, and through it would pass all men, provisions, garbage, and ammunition for the deck weapons. Everything apart from externally stored torpedoes would transit through this main hatch. The central area of the bridge itself was dominated by the housing for both periscopes: the maneuvering controls were situated at the bridge's front edge, next to a compass repeater and a voice pipe for use when communicating with the *zentrale*. The rotating shifts of watchmen would occupy the little remaining room that was available. To starboard, meanwhile, the Direction-Finding loop aerial was housed within a recess between the pressure hull and the boat's outer skin. As the War progressed, additional radar and radar-detection devices were fixed to the bridge, and to the outside of the conning tower. With the extra Flak guns installed to protect the boat from the air attacks that became an increasingly serious problem for the U-boats, it became necessary to enlarge the gun platform until it comprised two entire levels, sporting a formidable array of quick-firing weaponry.

Whatever the changes in appearance the bridge underwent over the course of the War, its primary function remained the same: to provide a platform for the watchmen. Whenever a boat was running surfaced, four pairs of eyes, occasionally augmented by the captain or an additional man to scan the sky, would be scouring the horizon for the tell-tale traces of enemy shipping. While at times mundane and dangerously monotonous, watch duty could also be extremely hazardous in rough seas. On several occasions, men were washed overboard from the conning tower. Some were lost forever, but others were more fortunate—as this brief entry from the War Diary of *U564* shows:

"April 7, 1942:

20:30 hours. Surfaced.

21:00 hours. Commander fell overboard.

21:14 hours. Commander fished out again, wet. Weather quite good."

Page right, clockwise from top left: The main helm within the control room, directly to the right of the forward hatch—the helmsman would sit at right angles to the two planesmen; U995's outer conning-tower hatch—the pedestal is for the UZO surface-firing targeting device, comprising heavy binoculars clamped to the rotating top which was, in turn, connected to the torpedo calculator; the navigation table, with beneath it the controls for the periscope and salvo-shooting combinations; the main navigation periscope, located in the control room.

Honoring fallen heroes

These tiny booklets commemorating lost *Wehrmacht* comrades were sold as Christmas-tree ornaments to raise money for "War Winter Relief Work" in December 1942. Günther Prien and Engelbert Endrass, who had been Prien's First Watch Officer, were both killed aboard their respective U-boats in 1941.

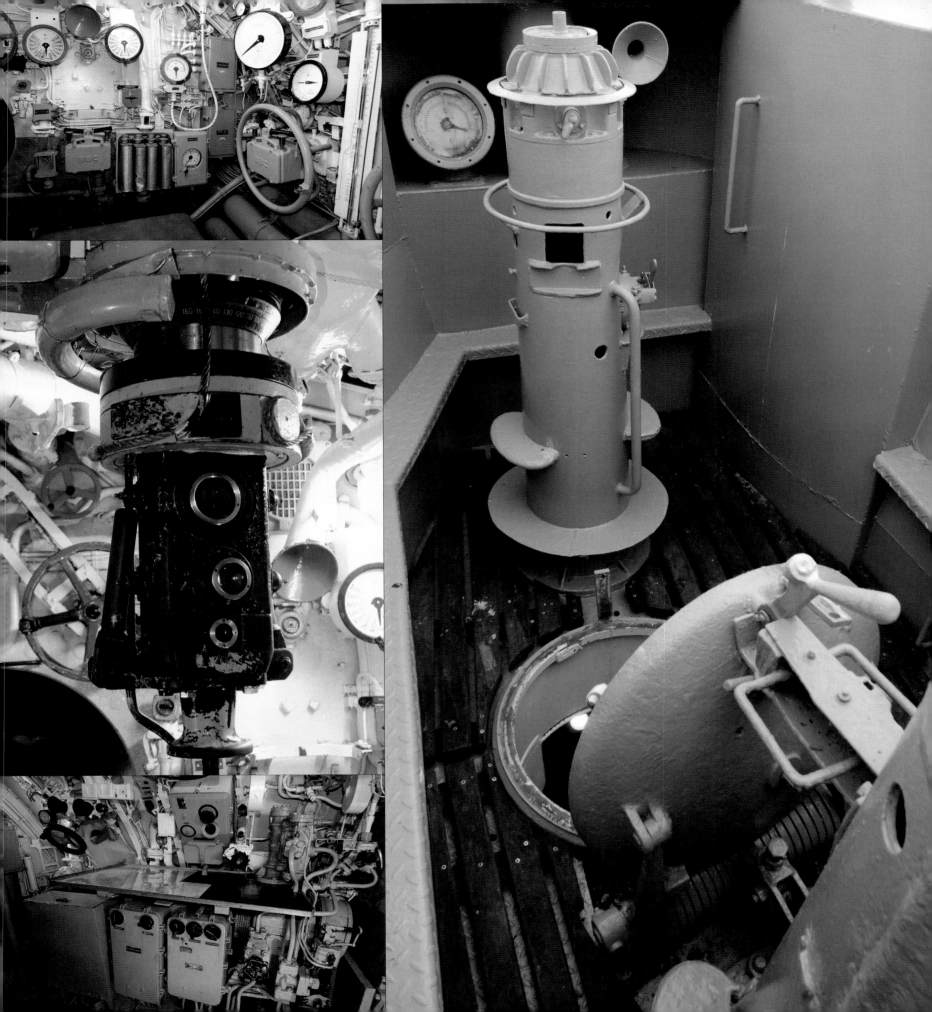

Washed from the bridge

Aboard *U653*, the *Obersteuermann* Heinz Theen remembered the loss of one of his boat's Watch Officers, along with his men, during particularly savage north Atlantic weather:

"*U653* left Brest [France] on February 10, 1943, on its sixth War Patrol. The operational area was to the east of Newfoundland. On the fourth day we had crossed Biscay with no problems or interference from the British, making a good fast passage. I had the morning period from 04:00 hours to 08:00 hours with my men of the Third Watch. During this watch the weather was becoming increasingly bad . . . The conning tower hatch was frequently deluged because of the heavy waves and the conning tower itself submerged, but always it climbed free again. My watch and I had had an easy first two hours, but the weather grew steadily worse. At the beginning we stood completely dry on the bridge, not even any spray coming over us. But by the end of our watch when the sea state had reached a strong 6 or 7 we were totally drenched. Then we shouted down to the next men of the First Watch that they would get 'somewhat wet' during their time on the bridge. These times were really 'shit weather.'

"The First Watch appeared dressed as seals [wearing heavy black raingear] at the time of changing over. I saw that the new watch was harnessed using their thick belts that were attached by a line to the tower. Then I handed the duty over to the IWO [First Watch Officer], Werner Laudon, after making sure that he too was correctly harnessed. I wished the IWO a good watch and he said to me, '*Obersteuermann*, I will try my very best so that in four hours the IIWO has better weather for when we change over. You weren't very successful at doing that for us during your watch! Enjoy your breakfast—at least you can dry out!' They were the last words that I exchanged with the IWO. I didn't know it at the time but I would never see him or his watch again.

"On February 13, at a little past 08:00 hours, over breakfast, I heard a loud noise coming from the control room when water flooded in from the bridge. The noise from the bilge pump and both diesels could be heard clearly throughout the boat. At 12:00 hours we were supposed to patrol with only one diesel to

Left: U995's bridge. It was cramped for the watchmen—and also dangerously exposed to the elements. The "mattress" aerial on the left is for the Hohentweil radar, introduced in 1944.

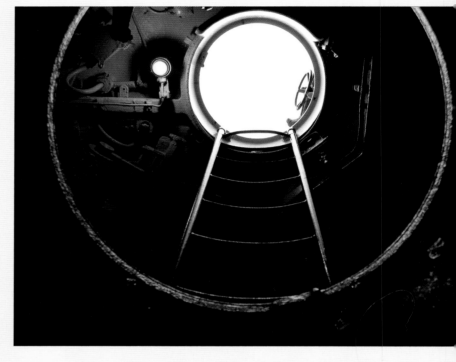

Above: *Looking from the control room through the conning tower to the open outer hatch. Survival could hang on the speed at which this ladder was negotiated.*

conserve fuel. Suddenly, at about 08:10 hours I heard no diesel noise at all. I went to the control room, where I questioned the *Zentralemaat*, Otto Tragesser, who explained to me that the air intake for the diesel had become submerged and was saturated with water.

"But within a minute the diesels sprang back to life. Jokingly, I said to Tragesser, 'The First Watch must think itself already ready for the change-over in three and three-quarter hours. These cruises are not always idyllic!'

"Subsequently, I had a look in the notebook that I had instructed the two *Zentralegäste*, Brand and Richert, to register course and speed changes into when I was having a break off watch or was asleep, in order that I had the documents to record what had happened for navigation. But Brand had forgotten, and I decided to start over again from when both diesels had stopped. It was irritating. He was relieved as I took the book back and began correcting it without saying a word.

"I had been in the control room for about five minutes by then when I noticed that the sound of rushing water, previously heard from above the control room, was now missing. The conning tower hatch was now closed. The *Zentralemaat* and helmsman inside the conning tower told me that the First Watch had apparently shut the hatch about seven minutes ago. I was puzzled and climbed up to open the hatch, and was startled to find nobody on the bridge. I could see no one from the First

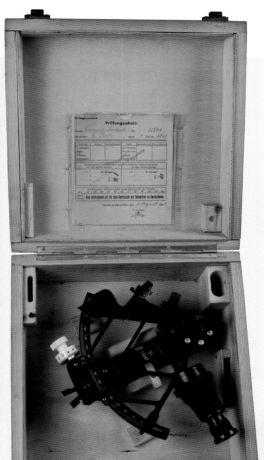

Above: A Kriegsmarine *sextant, issued in August 1944 but taken from a surrendered U-boat at the War's end.*
Below: *Sea boots were issued to U-boat men. The soles contained a cork lining for additional warmth.*

Above: *Padded, heavily insulated arctic underwear, suitable for northern climates.*

Watch. The bridge was empty! *U653* had spent seven minutes sailing blind. Despite well-fastened harnesses, four seamen had been snatched to their deaths by the cruel sea in an instant. By 12:00 hours we had searched for them but found nothing. Then the sea state got so bad that we had to abandon the search. After notifying BdU of the loss of our entire bridge watch we were told to carry on toward the front. BdU told the captain that replacements for the men could be transferred aboard.

"So *U653* sailed onward against England with only two bridge watches. During the Second Watch we combined some men from the Second and Third Watches with other crew and had some of the worst weather ever. Amazingly though, there was not one case of seasickness aboard like there had been on other patrols.

"The IIWO, Wilhelm Cranz, was a '*Neuling*' to *U653*—that is, it was his first patrol. Unfortunately for him, in his free time off-watch he had to stand in for the dead IWO. He was also supported very much by the captain. So, between watches, for about three hours at a stretch, he would come off duty and immediately 'listen to his mattress,' even if it was only for a short sleep.

"As *Obersteuermann* my first and foremost task was of course my navigation. By measuring distances on the sea map I was able to estimate the position of *U653*, helped by the recording of speed and course changes within my small notebook by the control room crew, Brand and Richert. Even today I have their names embedded into my head and I can't forget them as we worked together on the navigation. It would have been better to have been able to use my 'cutlery' [sextant], though.

"But morning and night I was unable to 'shoot the stars' as the heavy rain of the north Atlantic obliterated them. I was left only with the possibility of a sun sighting—but that was also unlikely! So, all during my free time I was always woken up by brief shouts of '*Obersteuermann*, the sun is coming out!' So I would run to the bridge at full speed with my sextant, whereupon the sun would disappear again. However, there were also—thank God—many times during the patrol when the sun would briefly appear, so that is how I spent lots of my free time, leaving about three hours of sleep a day."

Above: *Heavy-weather gear was worn in all but the calmest seas. In contrast to the heat and humidity inside the boat, the exposed watchmen had to face the cold and the sea itself.*

An escape and a rescue

U653 would experience at least some success during its sixth war patrol. Two ships had been sunk before the boat finally headed for home after six weeks at sea. On the way back, Heinz Theen recalled that **U653** located a large convoy—thanks to a cigarette—and then had a lucky escape:

"With two *Wimpeln* [victory pennants] being prepared for a total of 16,558 tons sunk, we began our return journey on March 14, 1943. There was only one defective torpedo left aboard, and we also were running low on fuel. On March 16, at about 03:00 hours, the Third Watch sighted convoy HX229. Today I can still remember the names of the watch—*Obermaat* Hein Scholz, *Matrosenobergefreiter* Dieter-Edmund Bönisch, and *Matrosengefreiter* Stemmler. They were with me when we all saw the convoy. This was, of course, in the time before radar replaced optical sightings [as occurred postwar]. They were given away by a cigarette, a single flame in the darkness that was seen. Then we looked around and saw that we were in the middle of the convoy. We dived.

"Throughout the afternoon we remained the contact boat. While we trailed behind, we sent beacon signals so that eventually several boats were in contact with the convoy. Also, the convoy SC122 was found by the gathering U-boats. Eventually, from both convoys, 21 ships totaling 141,000 tons were sunk—from a careless cigarette! But *U653* wasn't involved. We had in the meantime continued our journey home. From the supply U-boat *U462* we took more fuel and we reached La Rochelle on March 31. We left again and headed for our home port of Brest on April 2, and we were attacked in the pitch-black night by a two-engine enemy aircraft. I had the bridge watch, the sea state was 3 to 4, no navigation lights on. The Metox radar detector didn't utter a sound when the aircraft, at a range of about 2,000m [6,562ft], switched on a blinding searchlight, lobbing four bombs at us that all exploded in our wake. The depth was about 150m [492ft] so down we went, into an alarm dive. The new gear aboard the aircraft, the new radar that helped them hit U-boats, was probably not fully developed at that time. Good luck for *U653*!"

Above: *Made aboard U604, this photograph appears to capture the boat in a crash dive. The large-dial depth gauge—partially obscured by the navigation periscope—indicates shallow water, while the forward planes are set to maximum down angle. Speed was crucial in an emergency, as the boat was defenseless while diving.*

As Otto von Bülow, captain of **U404** explained, if possible the guns would be used in attacks, rather than torpedoes—to conserve fuel as well as torpedoes, both of which were highly valuable:

"At daybreak on June 1, 1942, about 300 nautical miles north-northwest of Bermuda, *U404* attacked the American freighter SS *West Notus* by gun fire. The risk in meeting an adversary with much superior artillery had to be taken due to a shortage of fuel, which would have been needed to attain an unseen forward position for torpedo launching. At that time of the War most freighters were armed, and had a trained crew against the little gun on our U-boats.

"Opening fire, *U404* had the good luck to hit the bridge with one of our first shells and flames quickly spread out. Very effective gunfire from a 13cm caliber was returned and there were several near misses. Splinters hit the sub, which was now running away at full speed, zigzagging. All of a sudden lifeboats were lowered and the ship was abandoned. While two boats were sailing away in good order, a third one manned by five men was full of water and motionless. One of these men, who turned out to be the first mate of the freighter, was requested to come aboard our boat. I welcomed him with a handshake and the words, 'I am sorry, but

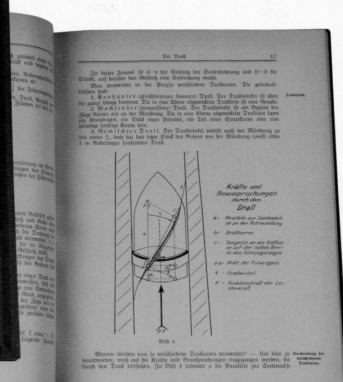

Left: *Diagram illustrating the spin achieved by rifling within the barrel of the U-boat's surface gun.*

Above left: *Issued to trainee officers, this book—Introduction to Artillery Lessons in the Kriegsmarine, Volume 1: Ballistics—provided novices with their first insights into the principles of surface artillery fire.*

Above right: *Stabsobersteuermann Karl Limburg, the navigator aboard U564, seen at his station. Limburg was already a war veteran, having enlisted in the Imperial German Navy in 1914.*

this is war. I hope it will soon be over and I am sure we will be very good friends.' We had a long conversation about ship and cargo, and the gun battle, while we were towing the damaged lifeboat toward the other boats that were under sail to hand over the mate and his men. Returning to the burning ship, we discovered another man hanging in a lifebelt, picked him up, and took care of his wounded leg then delivered him to the lifeboats undersail and now almost at the horizon.

"The rescue work was a matter of course and very simple humanity, but it may be of interest in the light of the propaganda against the Germans in those war times. I never heard any 'hurrah!' of the crew when a ship had been torpedoed and sunk."

Left: *Planesmen at their stations. Each station was provided with handgrips that allowed the planesman's hands to rest naturally, his palms in position over the push-button controls.*

Kretschmer's *U99* sunk

To survive, U-boat crews had to function as a team: every man had to know his task (or tasks), and perform it efficiently. Good navigation was essential to successful operations, just as vigilance on the bridge could avert disaster. Even the most experienced crews, however, could be undone by a moment's carelessness, as was the case for Otto Kretschmer and his *U99*. Kretschmer—the highest-scoring U-boat commander of World War II—remembered how his famous boat was finally sunk:

"On March 16, 1941, I was trailing the convoy HX112, after Lemp [*U110*] had discovered the convoy the night before, had attacked and then given exact position signals so that I could come down from the vicinity of Iceland. The weather was misty with bad visibility during the night. Therefore I had to dive, still on my southern course from Iceland, in order to find the convoy with my passive sonar. Lemp's navigation had been superb, so much so that I soon found myself in the midst of the convoy—ships all around me. So I surfaced, only to discover that I had popped up between a port escort and the first line of the convoy proper. Diving immediately, I let the convoy pass over me and surfaced at a safe distance to the rear, then trailing through the daylight of March 16 when the visibility improved so much that we could detect Sunderlands before they saw us. This meant diving and surfacing all of the time.

"On the starboard side of the convoy I could see two destroyers attacking a submarine underwater with depth charges. This made me change from the rear to the port side of the convoy to a surfaced station behind the horizon (as seen from the convoy). Knowing nothing so far of

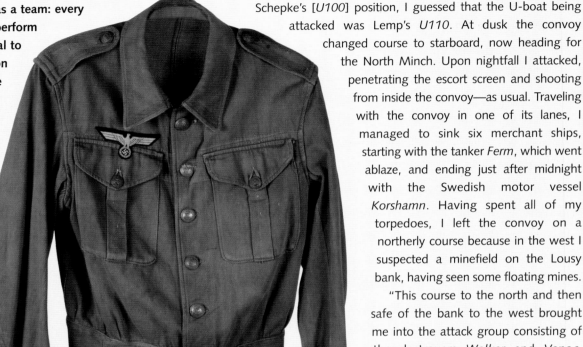

Above: *British denim battledress captured from BEF stockpiles in France during 1940, and converted for use by U-boat personnel.*

Schepke's [*U100*] position, I guessed that the U-boat being attacked was Lemp's *U110*. At dusk the convoy changed course to starboard, now heading for the North Minch. Upon nightfall I attacked, penetrating the escort screen and shooting from inside the convoy—as usual. Traveling with the convoy in one of its lanes, I managed to sink six merchant ships, starting with the tanker *Ferm*, which went ablaze, and ending just after midnight with the Swedish motor vessel *Korshamn*. Having spent all of my torpedoes, I left the convoy on a northerly course because in the west I suspected a minefield on the Lousy bank, having seen some floating mines.

"This course to the north and then safe of the bank to the west brought me into the attack group consisting of the destroyers *Walker* and *Vanoc*, under the command of Commander Donald McIntyre in HMS *Walker*, who was still chasing a U-boat that turned out to be *U100*. Through the fault of my starboard forward lookout, a petty officer, who had not seen anything of

Right: *An Allied merchant ship, its hull broken in two by torpedo attack. Despite the U-boats' continuing rise in fortunes in 1941, three of its "Aces" were lost: Günther Prien and Joachim Schepke, killed in action, and the "Tonnage King" Otto Kretschmer, captured.*

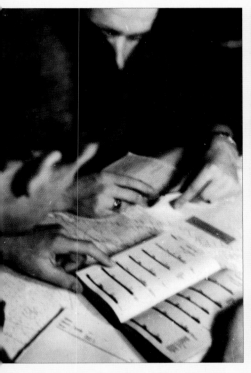

enemy's guns], but their 40mm Pom-Poms with their delicate anti-aircraft fuses only damaged my paint.

"I saw a destroyer [HMS *Vanoc*] with its broad silhouette lying at a short distance directly ahead of me. My engines were out of order, all my torpedoes had been spent earlier during the night . . . But if only I had had a single torpedo left I could certainly have sunk HMS *Vanoc*, the other destroyer having been farther away on my starboard quarter so that he could not have interfered. Of course I had some shells for the gun left, but with the list it was impossible to man it. The almost immediate firing of the destroyers made it also impossible to man the gun, which was enveloped by tracer shells from British Pom-Poms. Of course at that time I had no idea that *Vanoc* was about to pick up survivors from *U100*. Fate could have taken another turn . . . "

Below: *Despite efforts to identify valid targets, mistakes occurred. Mexican tanker SS* Potrero del Llano *burns after being torpedoed by U564 on May 14, 1942. Eight days later Mexico declared war on Germany, opening southern airfields to Allied aircraft.*

Above left: *Identifying target ships before, or even after, action helped paint a more accurate picture of U-boat successes at sea. But Dönitz's battle against merchant shipping would ultimately be lost.*
Above right: *Kptlt Reinhard "Teddy" Suhren astride the narrow saddle of the attack periscope in U564's conning tower.*

the approaching HMS *Walker*, we had almost run into the destroyer! Only the vigilance of the Watch Officer, who from time to time took a look around, covering also the petty officer's quarter, saved the boat from that fate. But unfortunately he sounded the diving alarm in contrast to my standing order not to dive in such a situation but rather to show the enemy the stern with high speed and call me onto the bridge.

"So, the boat became stationary in the midst of the hunting destroyers. *U99* got a full load of depth charges from HMS *Walker*, which effected an inrush of water, making the boat drop like a stone. Before the final crush—and with electric motors out of action—I managed to get the boat to the surface with compressed air, where she lay with a list to starboard in a pool of diesel oil. I couldn't get away because the diesels wouldn't do it either. Of course there were many waterspouts around my boat [from the

Attack!

"Dönitz taught an aggressive war—always attack! Nonetheless, the Battle of
the Atlantic was a grim but chivalrous warfare. The politicians make the wars and
the people have to fight them." —Otto Kretschmer, *U99*

**The procedure for torpedo attacks varied depending
on whether the U-boat was surfaced or submerged.
Early war doctrine advocated surface shooting so as
to take full advantage of the U-boat's high diesel
speed and slim silhouette.**

The tactic of slipping surfaced between escort ships
and attacking from inside the convoy body was used
to great advantage by such "Aces" as Otto
Kretschmer, Joachim Schepke, and Günther Prien. All
became famous in Germany during the first year of
the War. However, the introduction of radar negated
the advantage granted by their low superstructure,
and soon U-boats were forced to rely on submerged
attacks, firing at increasingly long distances and also
becoming more reliant on pattern-running and
homing torpedoes. As a result, U-boats were often
unable to stay and witness the outcome of attacks for
fear of detection by ASDIC, thus raising the number
of unsubstantiated success reports. Once submerged,
the U-boat was vulnerable due to its sluggish speed
and limited battery capacity, and if forced below by
the enemy it could be hunted to exhaustion.

Above left: *A still from a
propaganda newsreel made
aboard U552, and purporting to
show Kptlt Erich Topp in
action—however, the use of the
navigation periscope to launch
the attack makes this doubtful.*
Above right: *Timing the torpedo
run. Another still from the same
film. Topp is wearing British
denims; the lanyard whistle was
fairly typical issue.*

Left: *Controls beneath the
control room navigator's table
indicating pre-settings for single
or salvo torpedo firing.*

During a surfaced torpedo attack, the actual targeting and firing was handled by the IWO at the UZO (*Überwasserzieloptik*), or surfaced targeting device. Other lookouts were on hand to search for enemy threats, while the captain was always also present to maintain an all-round picture of the attack. The targeting instructions, such as target speed, angle-on-bow, and

distance, were passed verbally below to the interior of the conning tower, where the boat's Number One (*Oberbootsmann*) would program the necessary information into the torpedo calculator situated behind the ladder. This in turn passed the information electrically to the readied torpedoes, which were fired by hand on verbal instructions from the IWO. The *Oberbootsmann* shared the tower with the helmsman, who sat on a narrow ledge and responded to orders to change course that were issued via the voice pipe from the bridge.

Unfortunately for Joachim Schepke, one of the U-boat service's early leading commanders, his position on the conning tower of *U100* during a surface attack led to his death. While engaged against convoy HX112 in March,

1941, alongside Kretschmer's *U99* and Lemp's *U110*, Schepke was hunting surfaced while running on diesels. However, the British Royal Navy had at last perfected ship-borne radar and *U100* was the first U-boat to be successfully attacked after being located by radar. The destroyer HMS *Vanoc* detected the U-boat on an overcast night that would normally have prevented visual detection. Surprised, the U-boat was rammed as Schepke remained on the bridge, desperately trying to outmaneuver his attacker. The British ship's bow impacted against the conning tower, mortally wounding Schepke, whose legs were severed. *U100* sank and only six men survived to be picked up by the British.

Above: *Combat helmsman Matrosenobergefreiter Werner Grünert at his station inside the conning tower of U564. The boat is proceeding at "Slow Ahead," the voice pipes by Grünert's head passing instructions from the bridge.*

Left: Bootsmann *Heinz Webendörfer inputting information into the torpedo calculator, also inside the conning tower. This was an analog system that computed a firing solution based on data supplied, the solution being transmitted electronically to the torpedoes in their tubes.*

An emergency dive

The cry **"Alarm!"** would herald an immediate frenzy of action within the *zentrale* as the boat was thrown into a crash dive. This was the fastest method by which a U-boat could submerge. *Funkobermaat* Fred Geils remembered the order of events that would follow the command to make an emergency dive aboard *U373*:

"The first thing that followed the 'Alarm!' was for the bridge watch to come plummeting down the ladder. Then the conning-tower hatch would be slammed and the loud order 'Flood!' would follow. On my boat the order came as soon as the first of the men from the bridge had hit the deck. After receiving the emergency order the senior control room mate (*Zentralemaat*) would order exhausts closed, that is if the LI [chief engineer] was there he would instruct him to shut the exhausts while he made sure the men correctly carried out the order. After the order, the *Zentralemaat* would say, 'Exhausts closed, 5, 4, 3, 2, 1,' and then he would blow the diving cells using the main distributor panel. However, this could break down into confusion if not handled properly.

"I know aboard *U625* there was a lot of congestion in the tower with extra gun crews and a confusion of orders. On that boat, when it was in the north Atlantic during January 1944, they were attacked by aircraft.

Rather than 'Alarm!' the order 'Aircraft!' was heard from the bridge watch. So immediately the gun crew raced for the bridge to man the 2cm and 3.7cm cannons as well as some smaller machine guns. There, the guns were quickly manned and other men charged to the magazine to begin breaking out ammunition and passing it up for them. So there were also at least four or five extra people on the bridge and in the tower itself. When a second order— 'Alarm!'—was given, the Devil was let loose . . . With all the congestion in the tower, it led to the calamity of the captain being left outside as the boat dived, never to be found again.

"On my boat *Mechanikerobergefreiter* Günter Meyer had a brother, Fritz, onboard *U625*. They lost their captain on January 2, 1944, and enemy aircraft attacked us the next day not far away from their position. At 20:32 hours, six 113kg [250lb] Torpex depth charges were dropped on us as we crash-dived away from the attacking Wellington aircraft. One was a direct hit on the stern, near where the aerial joined the deck; although the bomb must have been damaged during the drop as it didn't explode, we were still damaged by it, and began leaking badly in the stern torpedo room. We surfaced as the water was over 200m [656ft]

Left: *Rounds of 88mm ammunition being lifted from the magazine, unpacked, and passed through the conning tower hatch.*
Below: *Daylight, and two crewmen, viewed from inside the control room.*

deep, and began shooting at the Wellington bomber. We had been outbound from Brest [in France] for Newfoundland, where we were due to operate, but now we couldn't dive we had to turn back. Every 15 minutes we released three 'Aphrodite' balloons from the tower. These balloons trailed strips of aluminum foil that provided a false radar echo and we hoped to distract our radar-equipped attacker with them. Sure enough, after one more attack that we repulsed with Flak, there were no more and eventually we made Brest again after a surfaced run. Once we were safely tied up to the pier at Brest, we examined the badly damaged outer hull and found that the unexploded depth charge was stuck there—and had been sitting there for 29 hours while we merrily brought it home. A special group of engineers were called to lever it out of its hiding place between the deck and the pressure hull, and defuse it, after which they took it away and blew it up. When the fuse was removed it was discovered that the reason it hadn't gone off was because it was set to explode at 70m [230ft], which we didn't reach during our last dive. The bang would have meant the end of us."

Left: *Type II* U9, *with extended* wintergarten, *diving into the waters of the Black Sea, where it saw action against the Russians.*
Below: *The ladder into the conning tower aboard* U995. *The large cylinder, with inspection hatch, houses the attack periscope well.*

U-boat watch duties

As with most naval craft, duties aboard a U-boat were divided into a series of watches. The *Kriegsmarine* had separate Line (Seamen) and Engineer/Technical branches. Most of the seamen branch was divided into three alternating watches atop the conning tower, each directly supervised by one of three Watch Officers. The First Watch Officer (IWO) was the boat's second-in-command, the Second Watch Officer (IIWO) was the junior officer aboard, and the Third Watch Officer (IIIWO) was the boat's navigator (*Obersteuermann*). Each of these watches was on duty for a four-hour shift.

The Engineering/Technical section, on the other hand, generally operated six-hour shifts under the supervision of their relevant section heads, such as the Senior Diesel Mechanic, Senior Electric Motor Mechanic (*Obermachinisten*), and Senior Radio Operator (*Funkmaat*).

For example, one 24-hour period would be divided as follows:

00:00 First Sea Watch and Starboard Engine Room Watch on duty.
03:45 Second Sea Watch woken.
04:00 Second Sea Watch on duty.
05:00 Cook woken.
05:30 Port Engine Room Watch woken.
05:45 Port Engine Room Watch breakfast.
06:00 Remaining Crew woken. Port Engine Room Watch on duty.
06:30 Breakfast for remaining free crew.
07:00 Clean ship.
08:00 Third Sea Watch on duty. Second Sea Watch breakfast.
08:45 Routine daily duties for men not on watch.
11:30 Lunch for First Sea Watch and Starboard Engine Room Watch.
12:00 First Sea Watch and Starboard Engine Room Watch on duty. Lunch for the rest of the crew.
13:00 Routine daily duties for men not on watch.
15:30 Snack for men going on duty.
16:00 Second Sea Watch on duty.
17:15 Evening meal for men not on duty.
18:00 Port Engine Room Watch on duty. Evening meal for Starboard Engine Room Watch.
20:00 Third Sea Watch on duty. Evening meal for those who have not eaten.
21:00 Lights out—silence throughout the boat for sleeping.
23:40 First Sea Watch and Starboard Engine Room Watch woken to get ready for duty at midnight.

Below: *First Watch Officer, Lt z S Hermann Neumeister, shooting the sun as* U281's *bridge watch continues to scan the horizon.*

Imprisoned underwater

Oblt z S Hans-Joachim Krug was IWO (First Watch Officer) aboard the largest type of combat U-boat to see action during World War II, the Type XB. For part of the eventful voyage, the boat traveled submerged for a marathon 168-hour period, and Krug vividly recalled the relief he and the crew felt when they were finally able to breathe fresh air again on the bridge:

"I was aboard *U219*, a 1,700-ton boat. Intended for mine-laying, its cargo capacity was so large that it was also used as a supply boat. So it was that in February 1944 we were filling the boat with cargo for a voyage to Penang. The *U219* had received some slight damage during its first operational patrol so was laid up for a period in Bordeaux, though by far the most preparation was given to rust treatment for this special mission, the longest we would be at sea not only taking supplies to our base in the Far East but also various articles of material for the Japanese. [After various mishaps, *U219* finally left Bordeaux on its supply mission in August 1944.]

"We finally departed for the Far East in August 1944. We sailed from the Gironde, and were almost immediately attacked by a Sunderland aircraft and some Mosquitoes. Another boat sailing alongside opened fire using Flak weapons with infra-red sights, but ultimately there was no damage to boats or aircraft. We dived after reaching the 200m [656ft] line.

Sure enough, our newly installed *Schnorchel* gear broke down almost straight away, but we kept going.

"In September we received an order from BdU to supply *U1062*—a Type VIIF minelayer heading back from Penang—in grid square EH7589, southwest of the Cape Verde Islands. Late on September 28 we surfaced looking for *U1062*, but found only the smell of diesel oil from the sea. During that afternoon we had already heard the sound of distant explosions. There was clear vision all around, the eastern horizon was dark, but to the west it was still light. We held a north-northwesterly course with all Flak weapons manned and the crew at action stations. All lookouts were desperately searching for *U1062*, but instead we saw aircraft. At 19:40 hours a lookout reported 'enemy aircraft, starboard aft.' Wrongly identified as Skua-type aircraft approaching with a red searchlight at a height of nearly 55m [180ft], the plane noticed us too late and overflew with no attack. But it opened its throttle and came in again from starboard abeam against the western sky. Eight 2cm and 3.7cm cannon opened fire as the aircraft released a bomb that shot overhead and exploded on our port side about 46m [150ft] away. The spray soaked us all on the bridge, but then I heard the cry, 'Aircraft on fire!' Sure enough, the plane ditches on our port side, trailing flame and smoke. The helmsman, situated in the conning tower, couldn't follow the orders shouted down the conning tower amid all the noise and put both engines to 'stop.' So there was more pandemonium as we know that other aircraft will come. But before we can crash-dive, the diesels need to be restarted. Finally, while diving, we heard strong explosions in our wake.

"We turned immediately to a southerly course and tried to leave the search area. After diving our hydrophones heard sonobuoys on the surface and a fanfare of noise, including depth charges. This continued throughout the next day. Some explosions [were] very close, others [were] further away as they hunted for us. I had the impression that surface ships and the aircraft were taking turns. The clock kept moving . . .

"Finally, on September 30, all was quiet and we surfaced to make a contact report to BdU. But there was

Above: *Men on U103 take the opportunity to bathe outdoors. On the left is the First Watch Officer* Oblt z S *Friedrich Markworth, the deep suntan he sports pointing to his role as part of the bridge lookout. During 1941, when this photo was made, enemy aircraft had yet to penetrate the central Atlantic.*

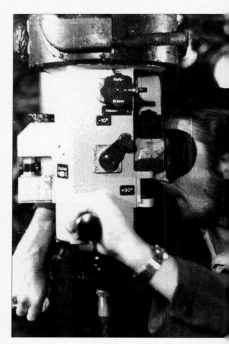

Above: Kptlt *Adalbert "Adi" Schnee of U201 using the binocular night-vision periscope, the NLSR (Nacht-Luftziel-Seerohr—night-sky search periscope).*

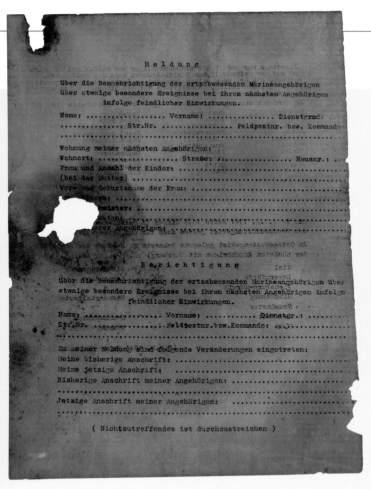

layers above the boat bounced the enemy's sonar emissions upward and we stayed down for a total of 69 hours. We had drifted about 193km [120 miles] during the long hours, while the enemy stayed behind and seemed to lose us. There were no more sonar echoes for one and a half hours, and on October 5 at 20:00 hours we surfaced in the middle of a dense sand cloud blown out from the African coast. It probably suppressed our radar echo. Most everybody came up on to the bridge, despite the sand . . . [we] were [all] close to fainting. A horrible stench came out of the hatch. The batteries were virtually flat and we were finally able to start the diesels and begin recharging them—the first opportunity for 168 hours!

"Well, we stayed submerged, except for four hours for battery charging, until we were south of Africa. We rounded the Cape of Good Hope in the 'Roaring Forties' just north of the ice drifts at 46° south, and entered the Indian Ocean."

Above: *Crewmen sitting on the partially submerged stern deck of a Type IX U-boat enjoy what appear to be warm equatorial waters. Any chance of fresh air and a sea bath was seized with both hands.*
Above left: *This standard form, to be filled out by crewmen, dealt with their personal effects and its shipment to next-of-kin should they become incapacitated. Ironically, this blank form was recovered from the wreckage of U352.*

no response, and within 18 minutes our passive radar detector picked up radar signals. Suddenly I was startled by a bomb splash behind us. We couldn't see or hear a plane, but we crash-dived and then were under almost constant bombing and were forced to stay down. Escorts came close to us with depth charges—they seemed to have found us but maybe did not have a clear echo.

"Hours and hours later, at around midnight on October 2, all was quiet and we surfaced. The radio personnel checked their antennae and found them all shorted out, the shafts leaking and soaked through. Radar signals again probed us and the radiomen had trouble getting back into the conning tower in a timely fashion as we crash-dived. Soon the sound of destroyer propellers was again overhead, followed by more explosions.

"We discovered that the boat could drift on a salinity layer with engines stopped. So the crew, to economize on oxygen, were all ordered to lie in their bunks except for the absolutely essential men. All machinery and every light was turned off, and we just had the glow of luminous paint and torches. The U-boat drifted with the current in a west-southwesterly direction. Other salinity

Left: *Kriegsmarine-issue sunglasses, minus their lenses. The glasses were shared by the rotating watchmen, and were flat so they could be used with binoculars.*

U-boat Emblems

The passion for painting images on conning towers began in 1939, when Fritz-Julius Lemp asked his radio operator Georg Högel—a talented artist—to paint an image of his dog on the tower of *U30*.

"It was not the first time we had had something on our tower. We had painted a slogan on our conning tower coming back from Spain during the Civil War, which was a quote from a speech given by Franco about the Battle of Santander. But Lemp loved his dog, 'Schnurzel,' and so asked me to paint him, which I did. Eventually we even had sweaters that bore Schnurzel on them."

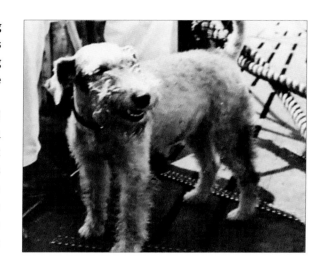

Left: Fritz-Julius Lemp's dog "Schnurzel," adopted by the crew as a mascot while in harbor. Lemp asked radioman Georg Högel—an accomplished artist—to paint an image of him on U30's tower.

by entire flotillas. Dönitz's theory—that the adoption of emblems fostered a sense of pride in the elite service—was correct, to the extent that officers carried their favorite insignia with them when they transferred between U-boats.

The variety of emblems and slogans was enormous—not least because many U-boats "adopted" by towns and cities in Germany displayed the crest of the location in tribute.

Inspired by this, the practice was adopted throughout the U-boat service. Although some staff officers were against it—they feared such emblems would enable the enemy to identify individual boats—Dönitz encouraged it, as he deemed it good for morale. With Dönitz's blessing, a myriad of emblems was then created. Some, such as Engelbert Endrass' "Snorting Bull of Scapa Flow" on *U47*, and Heinrich-Lehmann Willenbrock's "Laughing Sawfish," were later adopted

Interestingly, however, only 14 U-boats are known to have incorporated the Swastika in their emblems, at least one of which was included primarily for recognition purposes in the Far East.

As well as painting the conning towers, officers and enlisted men alike also began to wear personalized cap badges; some were made by the boat's engineering crew, others by professional badge-making firms. And what of the dog that had inspired Lemp in the first place? Sadly, Schnurzel's habit of greeting *U30* after each patrol made him a regular visitor to the docks, and as a result the animal was "adopted" by sailors from other boats. One day, he leapt aboard a destroyer leaving harbor. The vessel was bombed in error by the *Luftwaffe* in 1940 and sank—taking Schnurzel with it.

Above: Lemp and the "Schnurzel" motif on U30. Soon some of the crew were sporting sweaters with their chosen "logo," while others opted for simple cap badges.

Above: Cap badge for Neustadt's U-boat school.

Above: U161's green Viking ship.

Above: U592's Hamburg water carrier.

Above: *Cap badge adopted by crewmen of U294.*

Above: *Symbol of the Bremen City Musicians, adopted by U295.*

Above: *Triton graced at least two U-boats; this version was for the men of U172.*

Above: *U267's seahorse; U97 had been the first boat to bear this symbol.*

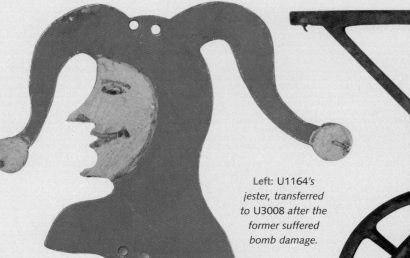

Below: *Ornate cap badge of the Officers' Crew XII/39, adopted by a member of this graduating class, Oblt z S Heinrich Meyer, for his boat U287.*

Above: *Symbol of the supply boat U462, the arms signifying help to other boats.*

Left: *U1164's jester, transferred to U3008 after the former suffered bomb damage.*

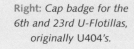

Above right: *The famous "Laughing Sawfish" of U96.*

Left: *U858 carried the emblem of the 100th Jäger Division.*

Right: *Cap badge for the 6th and 23rd U-Flotillas, originally U404's.*

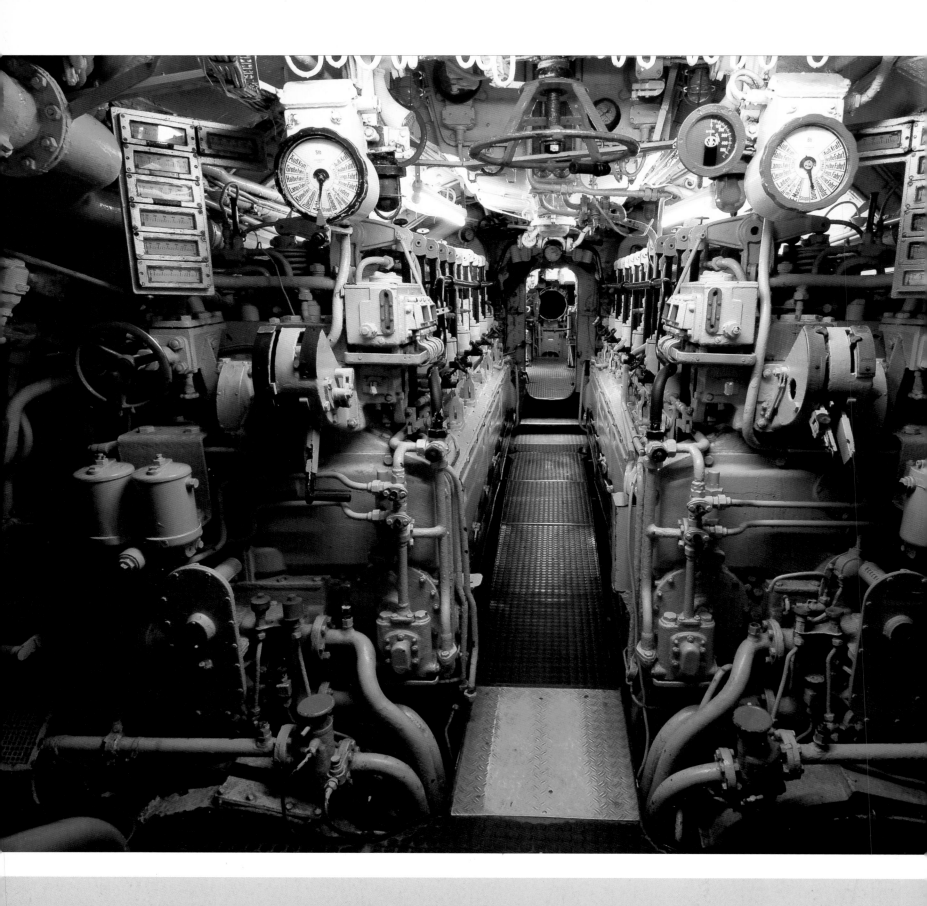

Diesel Engine and Electric Motor Rooms

"The heat and terrific noise—that was working the 'Jumbos.'"—Werner Banisch, *U260*

The main power plant for the U-boat was its two diesel engines. In Type VIIs, they were supercharged, 6-cylinder, 4-stroke diesels, generally manufactured by MAN or Germaniawerft. The engines were started by compressed air, which was stored in bottles above the pressure hull. The diesel room itself was situated immediately astern of the galley, from which it was separated by a watertight door. Two huge engines and their foundations dominated the compartment, which also housed oil pumps and coolers, a small workshop area and numerous valves for coolant, fuel, and oil. A narrow walkway stretched between the two engines, and this comprised the main working area for the "stokers," as the diesel crew were still called in World War II. There was very little space between the engines and the pressure hull. Overhead was a large holding tank for coolant water, as well as the air inlet control valve, which regulated the fresh air sucked into the compartment via trunking that led to an intake situated abaft of the conning tower between the pressure hull and the outer skin. Later in the War, air was brought in via the *Schnorchel*.

While the boat's LI (Chief Engineer) headed the technical division of the crew and was ultimately responsible for the smooth operation of the diesel engines, the chief diesel machinist (*Dieselobermaschinist*) was in direct control of the engines, assisted by at least one petty officer (typically a *Maschinenmaat*) and another two or

Left: Looking aft at the twin diesels aboard U995. The limited working space is evident from the narrow walkway leading to the open electric motor room door.

three lower-ranking "Lords." These men worked in an environment of noise and heat—the latter could reach extreme levels if the boat was operating close to the equator. Generally, the "stokers" worked in six-hour shifts, though this could be reduced to four at the discretion of the LI, if conditions within the compartment were thought too difficult. The physical effects of working the boat's "Jumbos," as the diesels were often known, included hearing loss, heat-related rashes, and boils, as well as reduced mental alertness (caused by an increased intake of carbon dioxide) and physical tremors and exhaustion—the diesels generated strong vibrations. The diesel crew rarely had time to relax, either: their skills were frequently tested, as they would often have to make running repairs while at sea, using the small range of tools and the limited space available to them.

Interestingly, Allied postwar analysis of U-boat development noted that the high surface endurance and surface speed of the U-boats was achieved primarily by stowing fuel in the main tanks, thus reducing the buoyancy reserve and surface sea-keeping qualities, restricting accommodation requirements to a bare minimum, and adopting the practice of allowing engines to be overloaded for short periods to achieve a maximum surface speed, something that came to be accepted practice.

Astern of the diesels and again separated by a bulkhead door was the electric motor room. This was manned by an *Elektro-Obermaschinist* who was assisted by a petty officer and two or three "Lords." The watch times were the same as for the diesel crew, though it is perhaps fair to say that duty in the quieter electric motor room was less trying than in the diesel room. The two units were drilled to work harmoniously together, as the time taken to switch from diesel engines to electric motors in the course of a crash dive could spell life or death for a U-boat. Unlike the larger Type IX U-boats, the Type VII motors were not separate from the stern torpedo area. Therefore the auxiliary helm, stern torpedo tube, *Bold* launcher, and compressors were also housed within this single compartment, though these will be dealt with later.

Batteries housed in two separate sections beneath the petty officers', warrant officers', and officers' compartments powered the electric motors. These battery banks comprised dozens of cells that were all vented individually, the separate piping leading to a common main air intake. This main trunking and the associated fans were also used for ventilation throughout the U-boat, being controlled with valves situated in the *zentrale*. The danger of this system

was that raised levels of hydrogen were to be found in the normal breathing air when the batteries were at full charge and freely venting gas.

To fully recharge exhausted batteries aboard a Type VII required between seven and eight hours at an optimum surface speed of 12 knots. This was achieved when one diesel was clutched to turn the propeller and the other to turn the electric motor, which acted as a generator for recharging purposes. This was the typical arrangement when recharging, although it was possible for both diesels to be clutched onto the electric motors, doubling the recharging rate but rendering the U-boat virtually immobile.

Page right, clockwise from top left: The main air inlet control valve, situated on the forward ceiling of the engine room; U995's port engine telegraph, distinguishable from starboard by the Bb—Backbord, or port— and the color red—as opposed to green and Stb, for starboard; the port electric motor; clutch and starter handle for the port diesel; the starboard engine telegraph.

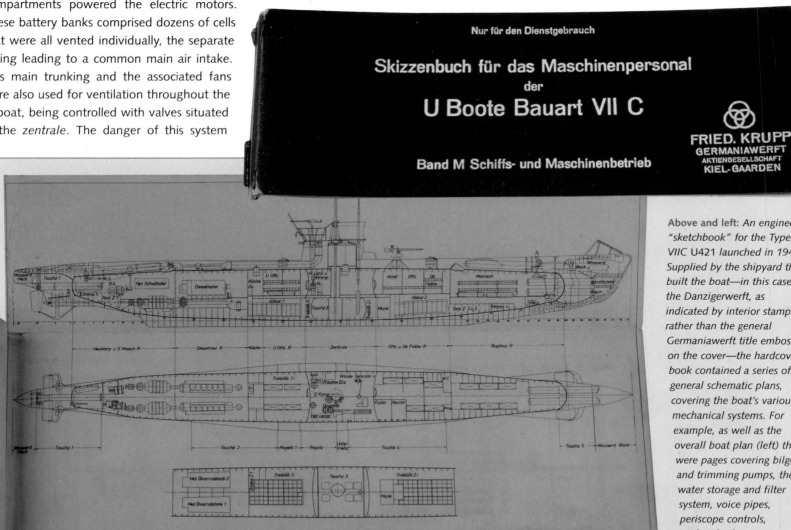

Above and left: An engineer's "sketchbook" for the Type VIIC U421 launched in 1942. Supplied by the shipyard that built the boat—in this case, the Danzigerwerft, as indicated by interior stamps, rather than the general Germaniawerft title embossed on the cover—the hardcover book contained a series of general schematic plans, covering the boat's various mechanical systems. For example, as well as the overall boat plan (left) there were pages covering bilge and trimming pumps, the water storage and filter system, voice pipes, periscope controls, and so forth.

U162's "cruel fight"

Maschinengefreiter Alfred Dietrich was aboard the Type IXC U162 during its last patrol in the second half of 1942. He described what it was like to be in the electric engine room during an attack by British Royal Navy destroyers:

"I went into the navy as a volunteer. The navy was made up of nearly all volunteers. I thought this would be a good way to develop my interest in being an electrician. The air force and army held no interest to me. I later volunteered for the U-boat service . . . My daily station on the U162 was the electric engine room. The technical crew was divided

Above: Maschinenobergefreiter *Walter Labahn (foreground) struggles to remove a cylinder head aboard U564 with the help of diesel* Obermaschinist *Hermann Kräh. Keeping the diesel engines in good working condition demanded constant attention from the on-duty engineers, and the ability to resolve any issues promptly.*

up into two watches, the starboard and port. We were four hours on and four hours off during the day, and six hours on and six off at night. When the Starboard Watch was on duty, the Port Watch was off. Each man also had additional stations like battle stations, diving stations, and maneuvering stations.

"In the late afternoon of September 3, 1942, [I heard] the engine telegraph ring to the diesel engine room for 'both engines full ahead.' A short time later came the command 'to diving stations' and with that came the alarm, a shrill bell ring. That meant both diesel engines would be shut down and the electric motors would go to full speed. Then the diving tanks would be flooded. Then came the command 'to battle stations!' There were three of us manning the electric motors. My post was now the

starboard motor. Instructions then came to shift to slow speed. The boat was about 60m [197ft] deep. The captain then came on the loudspeaker and said: 'This is the captain. A ship is coming. It is a warship, most likely a destroyer. We will attack.'

"The boat went up to periscope depth, about 14m [46ft], and then the command came to raise the periscope. Later, further orders came to prepare to fire a torpedo. The battle station began at 6pm and during the battle everything hinged on our hopes to be the victor.

"The torpedo mechanic in the stern torpedo room confirmed that a tube was clear to fire. The captain gave orders to fire and the torpedo shot out of the boat by air pressure and was on course for the

Above: Standard-issue canvas shoes with leather soles, worn by all the different ranks aboard U-boats.

destroyer. [But the attack failed. The torpedo "porpoised"—broke the surface—and was spotted by the destroyer, one of a group of three. U162 crash-dived.] The three destroyers were the *Pathfinder*, *Quentin*, and *Vimy*. They laid down a series of depth charges, trying to destroy us. It was a cruel fight. We developed a leak in the stern room. The U-boat listed about 30 to 35 degrees. We hovered like this at a depth of 200m [656ft], which was our limit. The crew tried to pump the water from the stern to the bow and then expel it, but was unsuccessful. We sank deeper and deeper: 200, 220m [656, 722ft]. We were sinking stern first. We had to hold onto something so that we wouldn't fall down. The heat was insufferable. I was bathed in sweat and my eyes were stinging. I was wearing only a pair of shorts and sailcloth gym shoes. My comrades and I in the engine room had our hands full. I kept busy at my post so as not to think about dying. The depth charges kept crashing above us. Glass bulbs shattered and the floor was covered with dirty oil coming from the diesel engine room. I kept thinking, 'I don't want to die. I want to live: I want to see my home and loved ones again.'

"Then we managed to stop the boat and actually head back up. We surfaced. There came the order to abandon ship. I grabbed my escape gear and ran through the diesel engine room on the way to the bridge.

I went quickly out through the conning tower to the deck. Waves were washing over the deck. I hung onto the 3.7cm cannon and put on my escape gear. The waves overcame me and from that point I never saw *U162* again . . . Thanks to the sportsmanlike efforts of the three destroyers and their commanders, all the crew from *U162*, except for two men, were rescued."

Paul Mengelberg was a diesel-room mechanic on *U26*—the only U-boat to successfully enter and leave the Mediterranean Sea during World War II. He talked about the ingenuity required to keep the diesels going while at sea:

"Members of the U-boat technical branch had to be very inventive. We had one time when we were forced to replace a piston pin

back in December 1939 on the bottom of the Mediterranean, which took us about 18 hours. It was a problem changing this diesel piston pin because the pin would not budge. So we couldn't get it out to change it. What to do? So, eventually we had an idea. The whole piston was removed and immersed in hot oil, then boiled on the cook's stove. Then we took it out of the oil, filled the hollow part of the pin with ice from the cook's ice box to shrink it just enough, and bingo, with a sledge hammer and a bit of luck the pin came out! The pot, however, would again have been used for preparing food, but was cleaned out before, of course."

Left: Maschinengefreiter *Alfred Dietrich of U162. Photographed in his blue service uniform, Dietrich sports his U-boat badge and the ribbon for the Iron Cross Second Class. Captured in 1942, Dietrich spent the remainder of the War in a PoW camp at Papago, Arizona.*

Above, left to right: *Standard-issue Kriegsmarine shorts. With the more relaxed dress code aboard U-boats—in contrast to that aboard surface vessels—men serving in warmer climates most* often wore shorts. The blue and white shorts were standard issue, while the khaki shorts were issued specifically for patrols in tropical climates, such as the Mediterranean and Far East.

Engine problems

Obermaschinenmaat Herbert Wien remembered how problems with the diesel engines while aboard *UA* ruined what had been thus far a successful patrol in the central Atlantic between June and August 1940:

"In the middle of the starboard engine's cylinder block we noticed a longitudinal crack leaking moisture. During low engine speeds the leakage decreased but never completely stopped. We were losing engine-cooling water. After a few days the same

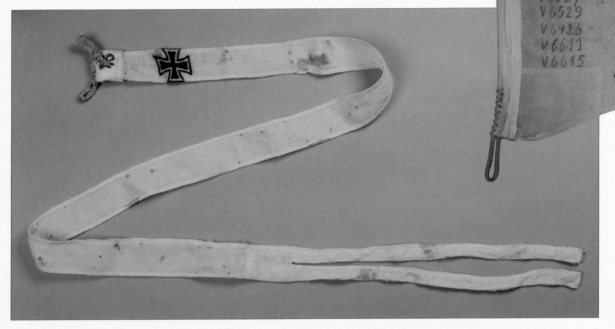

Above and left:
A Flotilla commander's pennant (above). U37 was the sole combat U-boat to fly it. The commander's pennant (left) would first be hoisted at the boat's commissioning and thereafter when transiting harbor.

thing happened on the port engine. The cause of the leakages on both engines was clearly rips that ran the length of the cylinder blocks. At higher engine speeds the cracks got wider and the stream of water increased substantially. But no one knew why!

"So, we had to decide, what could we do? These thoughts began to torment us—we were far from home, how could we make the distance without drive? . . . Some even spoke of heading to the nearest land and possible internment in the Canaries or Cape Verde but, thank God, it worked out differently. I'm not sure who came up with the idea, our LI or the diesel *Obermaschinist*. As it turned out, it was the torpedo-loading girder that came to our rescue. With a great deal of trouble, ability, and sweat, the T-rails that the torpedoes were clamped to during loading were sawn off and made into support girders. The cylinder blocks were then reinforced with these lashed on using wire rope and tightened with screws. The cylinder block fractures were probably not eliminated, but we were able to squeeze the blocks so tight that leakage was kept to a minimum. We could once again go at full speed. Besides, we had the possibility of adjusting the tightening screws during the whole return journey to rectify

any possible loosening of the clamping supports . . . With seven victory pennants on the periscope we reached home at the end of August in Wilhelmshaven. Here, surprisingly—and briefly—Admiral Dönitz came on board and saw only the standing engines, which looked fine when stopped. Only shortly afterward, a test run of the engines in Kiel in the presence of Vizeadmiral von Friedeburg and the Chief U-boat Engineering Officer *Kpt (Ing)* Thedsen showed the true picture of the last week's work that we had had to do. Our LI, *Kptlt (Ing)* Otto Teichmann received at that time a well-deserved Iron Cross First Class . . . For me, it was unfortunate that I was transferred from *UA* after this voyage as our experiences had 'welded' us together. I still don't know what caused the cracks, though I do know that *UA* went back to the Germaniawerft yards, where the engines were exchanged for new Blohm & Voss ones. Before the installation of the new engines, the entire engine foundations in the boat were strengthened—maybe that was it."

The introduction of the *Schnorchel* in 1944 finally allowed boats thus equipped to stay submerged for long periods during patrols. However, mastering the *Schnorchel* involved difficult procedures and, once in use, the device could cause discomfort to the crew and even create life-threatening situations, if handled incorrectly. However, the *Schnorchel* could also make the difference between life and death, as evidenced by

the end of *U260* in March 1945, as remembered by *Dieselmaschinist* Werner Banisch:

"Yes, I was aboard *U260* and took part in seven War Patrols as a diesel machinist. My duty post aboard the boat was the starboard diesel, obviously on the right-hand side of the boat, which I had to watch and maintain throughout the patrol. We had long hours on watch making sure the 'Jumbos' ran properly. But my main memory is from March 13, 1945. That date is very significant to me and I have always celebrated my second birthday on that date. Our crew only just escaped disaster.

"Our order was to attack British battleships in Liverpool. Of course we were informed of this at sea and not before leaving port. I think we were chosen because our boat got into the port of Reykjavik [in Iceland] some operations before. There, we had informed our leaders about American warships without attacking them with torpedoes. We were on our way toward Liverpool when the mine hit us near Fastnet Rock.

"It happened at a depth of 80m [262ft]—which was the regular depth for dangerous operations—so I was off duty at the time as we were running on electric motors. The mine destroyed the boat's bow and it dropped sharply forward toward the seafloor with the water that we were taking in. The outside hull had been destroyed and although the pressure hull wasn't totally holed, we were still leaking badly. We reached a depth of 192m [630ft]. Fortunately we didn't hit any rocks down there!

"Twice we tried to turn up tightly toward the surface, but we couldn't reach it. We ran the electric motors in full reverse and blew high-pressure air into the intact diving tanks. But every time that the boat was near the surface the air pressure inside the tanks was higher than the water pressure outside, and the air kept escaping the U-boat, water filled the tanks, and we would sink again. Finally the *Schnorchel* saved us. We had had it installed the mission before and used it between France and Norway—but we used it terribly! It was difficult, to say the least.

"With the help of the *Schnorchel* we started the diesel engines at a depth of about 14m [46ft]. [The diesels were usually only started once the head valve of the *Schnorchel* was in the air.] Once they were running, we channeled the exhaust gases into the diving tanks, which forced out the water and allowed the boat to become light enough to reach the surface. Our captain, Klaus Becker, headed for the Irish coast and we were able to hold her there for long enough for all of the crew to abandon ship into the life rafts. I was standing by the diesel engine throughout this time so I was one of the last ones to leave the U-boat. An eight-man lifeboat awaited me, but there were 11 of us! We rowed all night and reached the lighthouse at Galley Head as the first boat. So that is my second birthday!"

Above: *An array of extended U-boat masts—the* Schnorchel, *the combined radio-direction-finder loop and radar detector aerials, and the navigation and attack periscopes.*
Below, left and right: *Maschinenobergefreiter* Walter Labahn *of U564 changes a cylinder head, photographed by propaganda reporter PKMaat Haring.*

Ingenious engineers

Heat produced by the diesel engines aboard *U564* plagued *Kptlt* Reinhard "Teddy" Suhren, who, like all commanders, devoted as much time to the welfare of his men as to the boat itself.

"My longest journey as commander lasted three months. In between we stopped for diesel, which we received from a tanker, and also stocked up once again with provisions. One place in the Atlantic between the Small Antilles and the European mainland was still not covered by aircraft at that time [1942], so I gave the crew permission to go for 15-minute swims—in sections, mind you, so that just in case something happened we could quickly submerge. After the engines had been running at high speed we used to find it so hot in the Caribbean that even when we were underwater, the temperature of the U-boat rocketed, which made it very uncomfortable for the whole of the crew. Even then we made it possible to bring them all back to the mainland without having lost too much weight!

"We also made sure of hygiene, which was difficult. The men didn't receive a lot of water to wash themselves with. They grew beards, and none of that helped hygiene. So then our chief engineer, Ulrich Gabler, and his chief diesel officer decided that something had to be done. At the back of the diesel room one could remove the boards and into that space they built a bath, just big enough for one to sit in and also to have a shower. We were able to have a shower with the warm water of the engines' cooling system. In those days we had a sea-water soap from which one could get a good lather. [Interestingly, most U-boat men disagreed with Suhren about being able to get a good lather from this soap.] That was a marvelous idea! All we had to do now was check who was due, and then everybody received a liter [about 2 pints] of fresh water to finally rinse themselves off with. That paid off very well because the crew, even in this tremendous heat, felt more comfortable. We also had on board a fresh water producer, but it took one liter of diesel to produce one liter of fresh water from salt water."

Oberbootsmann **Max Schley, *U861*'s "Number One," talked about what it took to keep the crew motivated—and also the extra duties the mechanics and engineers were required to perform to achieve this, over and above keeping the engines running.**

"Many people are particularly interested in what I did every day aboard the U-boat. The largest amount of my time was taken up with watch duties. Naturally, this is not to forget the daily cleaning of the U-boat. Any classes held aboard the boat were still given as usual, and it was our doctor who dealt with the ones that particularly covered health and safety during our impending stay in the Indian Ocean and ashore. These talks were successfully given in the stern room, and so by January 1945 the crew were healthy for their return journey. But organizational and technical matters were also demanded during this voyage. For example, the

Above top: *Taking advantage of calm seas—and with no enemies in sight—a crewman washes al fresco.*
Left and far left: *Minimal mid-Atlantic aerial threats before 1943 meant more time spent on deck; Walter Labahn uses Ulrich Gabler's ingenious shower arrangement aboard U564.*

engineers had all kinds of things to manage. The fresh water producer was active day and night. Not least because our batteries required a certain amount of distilled water. Often the producer would fail. Then our electrical *Obermaschinist* and his men would have to fix it. Also, the preparation of our food took a certain amount of water too. Plus at morning and evening meal times the crew needed some water to drink. Additionally each man got half a glass of water to brush his teeth with. So, it took time to successfully manage all of these things and also required a great deal of self-discipline and comradeship between the crewmen, so that every single man received his allotted ration of drinking water."

A failure in electrical systems, meanwhile, could render a U-boat utterly helpless if submerged—the boat relied on salinity layers and exact trimming to keep it at a level depth. The crew had to be able to think quickly to solve such problems if disaster was to be avoided, as related by Reinhard Suhren, captain of *U564*:
"Part of our training was to insure the entire crew was prepared for any possible equipment failure. We once experienced a complete electrical circuit failure after being attacked with depth charges. It is difficult to explain just how complex— and also how simple—the problem actually was.

"There are switches that one turns to connect the battery to the live circuit. These were mounted on two boxes and as we looked at them by flashlight we saw that the indicator wheel was still pointing to 'On.' So, we didn't know what was wrong. But that was when an idea occurred to the LI. He took the wheel out and noticed that the blades had actually fallen out, but that the wheel hadn't turned. So, by replacing the blades and inserting it once more the problem was solved, and our electricity was restored. On other occasions something might happen for which you had received no training; or, when under depth-charge attack, [we were kept busy] trying to guess what the commander will do. One will say to go to 150m [492ft] and that that is the right depth, another would say 180m [591ft] is the right depth. They used judgement, which could not be taught but only learned."

Above: *Before Allied aircraft had begun to "blanket" the Atlantic, sunbathing and swimming gave some relief from the damp and unhygienic conditions, and the lack of natural light, which caused such health problems for Germany's submariners.*

HARTMANN & BRAUN
A-G   FRANKFURT/MAIN   H&B

GEBRAUCHSANWEISUNG

Left: *A sturdy leather case with equipment for testing electrical circuits. The manufacturing company Hartmann & Braun AG had been providing electrical components and associated equipment since 1879, and was one of the leading suppliers of such finely tuned testing devices for the Kriegsmarine.*

Refueling at sea

"By being able to take on fuel and torpedoes the U-boats could stay at sea off America where, for a while at least, their hunting was good."—Ludwig Stoll, *U148*

With U-boat operations ranging to the coast of the US in 1942, and eventually as far as New Zealand, it became essential to be able to refuel at sea. Certain U-boat designs were built specifically to cater for the demands of extreme long-range patrolling, namely the Type IXD2, which traveled to the Far East. However, Dönitz's onslaught against the US was originally waged with only six of the long-range Type IXCs, and this force had to be augmented with smaller, medium-range Type VIIC U-boats. Thus the issue of at-sea refueling became critical.

Early in the war, U-boats had used neutral ports in Spain and the Canary Islands to refuel covertly—Spain's fascist leader General Franco, though unwilling to commit openly to the Nazi cause, remained sympathetic to Germany and was willing to render secret assistance. German supply ships had been "interned" in Vigo, Cadiz, and El Ferrol on the mainland and at Las Palmas in the Canaries, and they supplied the U-boats with torpedoes, maps, food, and diesel fuel (they also treated wounded crewmen). However, these operations ended completely by 1942 after diplomatic pressure was brought to bear on the Spanish by the British, who were aware of Franco's covert aiding of the Nazis.

Regardless, the location of these tankers did little to assist U-boats in the western Atlantic. Instead, U-boats began to transfer fuel between themselves as those that arrived on station were able to take a carefully calculated amount of diesel from U-boats beginning their return voyage. This was one advantage of the tightly controlled nature of U-boat operations, with each boat required to report periodically to BdU while at sea.

At U-boat command there was therefore an accurate picture of how much fuel each U-boat possessed, and any lacking sufficient quantities could be directed to other boats known to have a surplus. In March 1942 the first of ten *Milchkuh* Type XIV supply U-boats began

Above: The long-distance Type IXD1 U-boat U195 in the warm equatorial waters of the Indian Ocean.
Above left: Refueling at sea; the fuel line can be seen trailing between the Type XIV resupply U-boat (foreground) and the receiving boat.

Right: Headlines announce the arrival of U-boats in the Caribbean Sea in 1942, and the shelling of the "world's largest oil refineries."

Far right, top: *Crewmen enjoy a feast of bockwurst (a type of German sausage) on the bridge of U861 as the U-boat approaches Penang, in Malaysia.*

operations. Occasionally, larger U-boats had been pressed into service in the past as makeshift dedicated tankers in support of combat boats, but now for the first time Dönitz had purpose-built supply U-boats. Each *Milchkuh* carried a doctor who was well equipped, an onboard bakery, a large deep-freeze compartment, machine shop, spare crewmen, and, crucially, food, fresh water, spare parts, ammunition, and 720 tons of spare diesel. With these boats at sea the Type VIICs became regular features of war within the Caribbean and even as far as Brazil.

The act of refueling at sea required the transfer of a floating hose—filled with air from a compressor that served as buoyancy but also to flush the hose after each use—from the supply boat, generally streamed behind as it proceeded slowly. This hose was hauled aboard the receiving boat, and the transfer of fuel would begin. Needless to say, both boats were extremely vulnerable to attack at this time.

Eventually, the Allied forces specifically targeted the tanker U-boats. Because they had cracked the Enigma codes, they were able to learn when refueling meetings were scheduled, and thus to attack both U-boat and supply boat when they were at their most vulnerable. By June 1944 the last of the *Milchkuh* had been sunk. The Germans belatedly developed techniques for refueling while submerged (when they would be safer from air attack), but it was imperfect. It thus proved impossible to maintain the presence of the Type VIIC in distant waters.

Right: *Alongside the routine transfer of goods from supply boats, unused torpedoes, food, and water were all regularly exchanged between departing U-boats and those arriving at the front.*

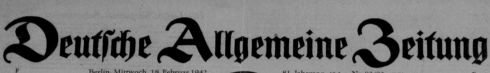

The end for U732

Claus-Peter Carlsen's *U732* was heading for the Mediterranean in October 1943 when it was depth-charged by the armed trawler HMT *Imperialist*, causing it to sink down as far as 178m (584ft). Although the engineers and mechanics kept the engines working, a disastrous sequence of events in the engine room led to the final demise of the boat and capture, or death, of the crewmembers.

"We were detected by the trawler which brought us to the surface with depth charges, where we came under fire. We sank back down again out of control and finally hit the bottom, where the engineers tried their best to get us back in shape. The enemy thought they had destroyed us, and they nearly had. We were afraid of gas, and the boat was full of smoke and fear as the LI got to work with his mechanics. I still have dreams about this now.

"But we managed to get back to the surface though we only moved slowly, with a strong list. The diesels were still working and that was the main thing. But they found us again. This time it was a destroyer searchlight and we came under fire and were hit. The engines were still working but we had had it, the boat was holed and was going to go down. So I ordered the men out . . . [most of the crew] climbed into the tower and jumped over the side while the rest waited with me on the bridge. But then the destroyer fired into the group of swimming men and I saw some of them hit, but then the searchlight blinded us and I could only tell the rest to get off the boat. We had the front planes blocked in the upward position. We were still moving at high speed and the bow was sticking out of the water. Everything below was flooding and because the diesels' air intake finally submerged, cutting off the air supply, the engines stopped and the boat sank beneath us. At this moment the destroyer started firing into the water again. There were also still depth charges being thrown. Then I also heard another noise—a battery explosion. It is a chemical process aboard my boat. Flooding of the batteries produced gas, and then a spark and the boat explodes. I was glad that it actually exploded because it meant no one could reach my boat. It was tragic, but I was also relieved.

"With my LI, I was struggling in the water. There was another man near us who couldn't blow up his jacket, so we helped him and told everybody to stay together, but there was still firing until I saw the destroyer lower a lifeboat at last. At that point I said that I would not go aboard the ship that has killed so many of my men. I will try to swim as long as I can toward Tarifa, Spain, as I know this area due to cadet training aboard the cruiser *Emden* when we were there before the War. I started swimming and after about five or six hours I was still going well in my life vest, which was holding my head up. I had seen my remaining men picked up and tried to get away. But after this time I lost consciousness, woke up again, and saw a ship with the Swiss cross on the side and flying a Portuguese flag. I blew my whistle and they sent a boat to pick me up. I remember when they heaved me onboard and then the next thing I woke up in a bunk. A Swiss

Above and left: Such very severe bomb and gun damage could be sustained, just so long as the all-important pressure hull remained intact.

Top of page: Early U-boats carried an emergency phone buoy like the one aboard the Type XXI U3008, seized and put through trials by the US Navy.

man was sitting there and he told me his name and that they were taking post from Egypt to Portugal, so I thought, this is very nice. Two or three days in Lisbon, I will be back in France and get a new boat. But a destroyer had seen this, too, and the next morning I heard aircraft, and then the Swiss man came back to tell me that we were being boarded by an English crew and there was nothing they could do. So, I was later sent to Gibraltar and my war was over. There the rest of my crew was too, but we had lost 31 men."

Above: *The* Tauchretter *escape gear, made by the Lübeck firm, Dräger, was issued to all U-boat crewmen, primarily for reaching the surface from depth.*
Right: *An engineer's leather jacket—with its distinguishing truncated collar—and standard U-boat lifejacket, complete with oral inflation tube, whistle, and, for rapid inflation, a compressed-air canister.*

To the Far East

Kptlt Jürgen Oesten commanded *U861*, the large Type IXD2 that traveled from Germany to the Far East and back. Replacement parts and material for the engines and electric motors were only two of the many logistical problems faced when they were so far from home.

"I went to the Far East in 1944 as by then I had been a staff officer for some time and had had four different admirals in charge of me during my period with *Admiral* Nordmeer in the northern end of Norway. From these four, Schmundt, who was an aesthetic man, he was the best. *Konteradmiral* Klüber—well, his nickname was Mr Dunlop because he was so far up his superiors' arses that you could only read the Dunlop on the heels of his shoes! So, I asked for another combat posting. My last boat was a Type IXD2. It was a longer edition of the old Type IXB and had a long range, 32,000 nautical miles. This was only possible because we had eight diving cells and at the start of the journey we were floating on only three cells, with the rest full of diesel fuel. That was the only way we

Left: *Useful phone numbers for German personnel stationed in Singapore as part of the late-War U-boat presence in the Indian Ocean.*

Above: *Tropical mess jacket for a* Fähnrich, *complete with the ribbon for the Iron Cross Second Class, but without the metal breast eagle.*

could happily reach Japan. We could reach Penang without having to refuel. On the contrary, when we returned from there we carried some cargo in some diving cells and still had enough fuel to refuel another boat about 1,600km [1,000 miles] south of Madagascar and still reached home. But they were very slow to dive, the large flat plane of the deck interacting with the surface of the water and leaving the boat 'hanging' there. It took at least 36 seconds to get off the surface and even that was only possible using every trick I knew. Plus, all of these boats had about 20 or 30 tons of surplus weight in the boat. You see, if the boat is underwater you have to correct her trim for neutral buoyancy. But on the surface you had this surplus weight in water in tanks, which you blew out

at the moment of diving in order to improve or accelerate the dive. But the diving time was unnecessarily long and a moment of great danger. Of course we had the advantage of extra space for torpedo storage tubes under the deck and so on, but that was no real compensation.

"On September 2, 1944, *U861* celebrated its birthday—one year in commission. So I thought I would give the crew a treat, so I went into a small atoll, Aldabra Islands north of Madagascar, and so we went in there and entered the lagoon, ready to launch the dinghy and let men go ashore onto dry land in small groups. The temperature inside the boat was very high and it would do the men from the engine rooms in particular some good to get the sun on their backs and stretch their legs. But shortly after arriving a Catalina aircraft flew overhead. I later found out they were just on a transfer flight and not keeping a proper lookout, in what they probably thought were fairly safe waters. So, as they flew by, we had all of our guns trained on them—one 10.5cm, one 3.7cm gun, and four 2cm guns, all of them tracking the aircraft. But

Right: *Guidebook to Singapore ("Syonan," to the Japanese) issued to U-boat men, with a Japanese pass allowing dockyard access.*

they didn't see us, so we said, 'Alright, let them go!' because we had just gone into the lagoon for fun, there was no military reason for it. But unfortunately it didn't work anyway as the current in the lagoon was so heavy that we had to recall our rubber boat so no one reached shore.

"Once we had reached Penang we rested for some time and then were later transferred to Singapore. There, we could overhaul the machinery and then we headed on to Surabaya because the Dutch had built a good dockyard there. Using these facilities we were able to exchange the cargo stored within the ballast keel. We had about 120 tons of mercury in bottles stored within the keel, which we gave to the Japanese in exchange for loaded tons of concentrated iron ore, a special metal compound needed to improve the quality of steel in a way similar to tungsten. Then we left in January 1945 for Norway. Later the British unloaded that cargo for us, as by the time we arrived the War was very nearly over.

"Although a great deal of Japanese manufactured parts did not have the required high specifications that our German machinery needed, we didn't really have too much trouble with obtaining fuel and food in Penang, and so on, as anything we couldn't have within our own stores we often managed to obtain on the Chinese black market.

The Japanese couldn't afford to shut down that black market as they relied quite heavily on it themselves.

"Another quirk of the Type IXD2 was that we carried the *Bachstelze* aboard our boat, stored in parts within canisters on the aft end of the *wintergarten*. There was a platform where it was assembled and a pneumatic winch with which it was tethered. If there was enough wind it could be launched with the boat stopped, but if not, then we had to be moving as the machine had no power. It was a glider—a gyrocopter. We had four boys aboard *U861* who had been trained to use it, although anybody who could handle it could have worked it. On the way home from the Far East we actually sighted a ship using it, but by the time we had winched it in and begun the chase they gave us the slip. I reported to Berlin that I had seen it with the help of the *Bachstelze*, but had had no success."

Far left: *Closing vents in the diesel engine room prior to diving; in the center is the main engine air inlet, the others being for the room itself.*

Above: *U511 arrives in Penang on July 20, 1943. Designated "Marco Polo," U511 was handed over to the Imperial Japanese Navy for tests and evaluation.*

Stern Torpedo Room

"We were instructed to keep the stern tube loaded with a T5 homing torpedo; BdU wanted us to keep the 'sting in the tail.'"—Gerhard Buske, *U223*

The final area within an operational U-boat housed the stern torpedo tube, or tubes. In larger U-boats, such as the Type IX and XB, this was a separate compartment. Although those boats possessed only two tubes in the stern torpedo compartment, it was similar in function to the bow-room, serving as extra quarters for the large crew, as well as a weapons station. Within the smaller Type VII, however, there was no such compartment. The stern torpedo section was simply the aft-most portion of the compartment that housed the electric motors. But even within the same design series there were numerous variations: some Type VIICs—*U203*, *U331*, *U351*, *U401*, *U431*, and *U651*—had no stern tubes at all, as there were parts shortages when they were being built. Similarly, the ten Type VIIAs (*U27* to *U36*) with which the *Kriegsmarine* entered the War had no interior stern torpedo tubes but were instead equipped with one torpedo tube mounted externally, on the deck. (This meant in turn that the VIIA's tube could not be reloaded at sea; furthermore, because the torpedo was exposed to the elements, the distilled water that was used to produce steam in its engine froze solid during the cold winter months, rendering the entire device useless.)

Despite the deficiencies, the Type VII design had shown enormous promise and was further developed into subsequent versions. The position of the VIIA's single, large rudder precluded moving the external tube into the boat, so the VIIC was built with double rudders. This allowed for the single tube to be placed lower down to

fire between the two rudders, which also improved the boat's maneuverability. The internal tube also made it possible to carry a spare, reload torpedo between the two electric motors and, toward the beginning of the War, another reload torpedo was accommodated in an external tube under the upper deck. This, however, had to be manhandled into the boat before it could be used. With these improvements, the VIIC was to become the biggest submarine class ever to be produced.

Alongside the torpedo-firing station for its single tube (in Type VIIBs and Cs), the stern area also housed the auxiliary helm. A large wheel, the auxiliary helm was secured to the port side when not in use; in an emergency it could be swung into position and used to control the rudders directly. No compass was provided in this section, only a simple helm indicator, and so directions would be relayed from the control room.

The U-boat's compressors were also astern. The main diesel-driven Junkers high-pressure air compressor was situated to starboard, while the auxiliary electric-powered compressor was located on the port side. The compressed air that was stored in a number of small tanks was used to launch torpedoes, and to start the diesel engines, while the air stored in the larger outboard tanks was used to blow the tanks in emergencies. These exterior tanks were vulnerable to damage and were regularly checked for leaks that could betray the position of a submerged boat.

Another feature of the stern compartment was a revolutionary new device inspired originally by Adolf Hitler. On September 28, 1942, Hitler and senior *Kriegsmarine* officers, including Dönitz and Raeder, engaged in conference in Berlin's Reich Chancellory. While

Left: U995's stern torpedo room. The single stern torpedo tube dominates this aft part of the compartment, which was shared with the electric motors, visible in the foreground.

The German Cross

On September 28, 1941, Hitler created the *Kriegsorden des Deutschen Kreuzes* (War Order of the German Cross)—shortened to *Deutsche Kreuz*, or DK. Hitler had wanted the new decoration to be called the "Order of the Swastika," but *Wehrmacht* leaders opposed this overtly political title. The new medal was awarded for performance over an extended period, rather than for a single act of valor. It was issued in silver and gold—the color of the central wreath. Between the Iron Cross First Class and Knight's Cross in status, it was nonetheless an independent award. Pictured is the cloth version of the German Cross in Gold, for attaching to a service uniform where the large and weighty metal decoration could not be worn.

Page right, clockwise from top left: *The wheel for equalizing pressure within the* Bold *decoy launcher aboard* U995; *the large wheel of the emergency helm, secured to port when out of use; the open stern torpedo tube—to the right can be seen the black metal piston fitted behind the loaded torpedo, allowing compressed air to push the torpedo from the tube; pressure dials on the Junkers compressor, located to starboard within the stern compartment; door from the diesel room, marked "Stern Torpedo and E-Machine Room."*

Hitler expressed a keen interest in the general state of Germany's U-boat war, he was strongly motivated by a desire to monitor and discuss technological advances that would aid Dönitz's struggle, particularly high-speed submarines, homing torpedoes, and improved explosive shells. Furthermore, Hitler expressed a desire for the development of a "decoy torpedo" that could simulate the destruction of a U-boat when under attack. His original opinion was that special torpedoes carrying oil and various items of wreckage could be carried and launched in the event of a prolonged hunt by enemy destroyers. However, the loss of an operational torpedo tube for the carrying of such a device was unacceptable to U-boat officers, although some did suggest that perhaps oil and air could be stored in an on-deck canister for release in an emergency. However, this too was swiftly proved to be impractical—due in no small part to its vulnerability to depth-charging that could provoke an unplanned release that would betray the U-boat's position to the enemy.

Nonetheless the idea had considerable merit and a compromise design resulted in probably the most effective of the German anti-sonar counter-measures. Named *Bold* (short for *Kobold*, meaning "deceiving spirit" or "goblin"), this device comprised a 6-in (15-cm) diameter capsule filled with 13oz (370g) of calcium and zinc that was expelled from the stern compartment of a U-boat through a purpose-built ejector (named the *Pillenwerfer*—"pill-thrower"—by crewmen). The calcium-zinc compound was packed within a wire mesh bag, which was in turn stored inside an aluminum canister. This waterproof canister carried a hydrostatic valve that controlled the entry of seawater. Upon contact between the leaking water and the stored compound, hydrogen gas was produced, resulting in a large mass of leaking and expanding bubbles that resembled the ASDIC echo that was produced when a submarine was detected by a ship on the surface.

The hydrostatic valve regulated the entry of seawater to such an extent that the *Bold* capsule could continue to emit bubbles for up to 25 minutes. Thus, while not simulating the destruction of a U-boat as originally envisioned, it became the first functioning decoy weapon, derivatives of which are still in use today.

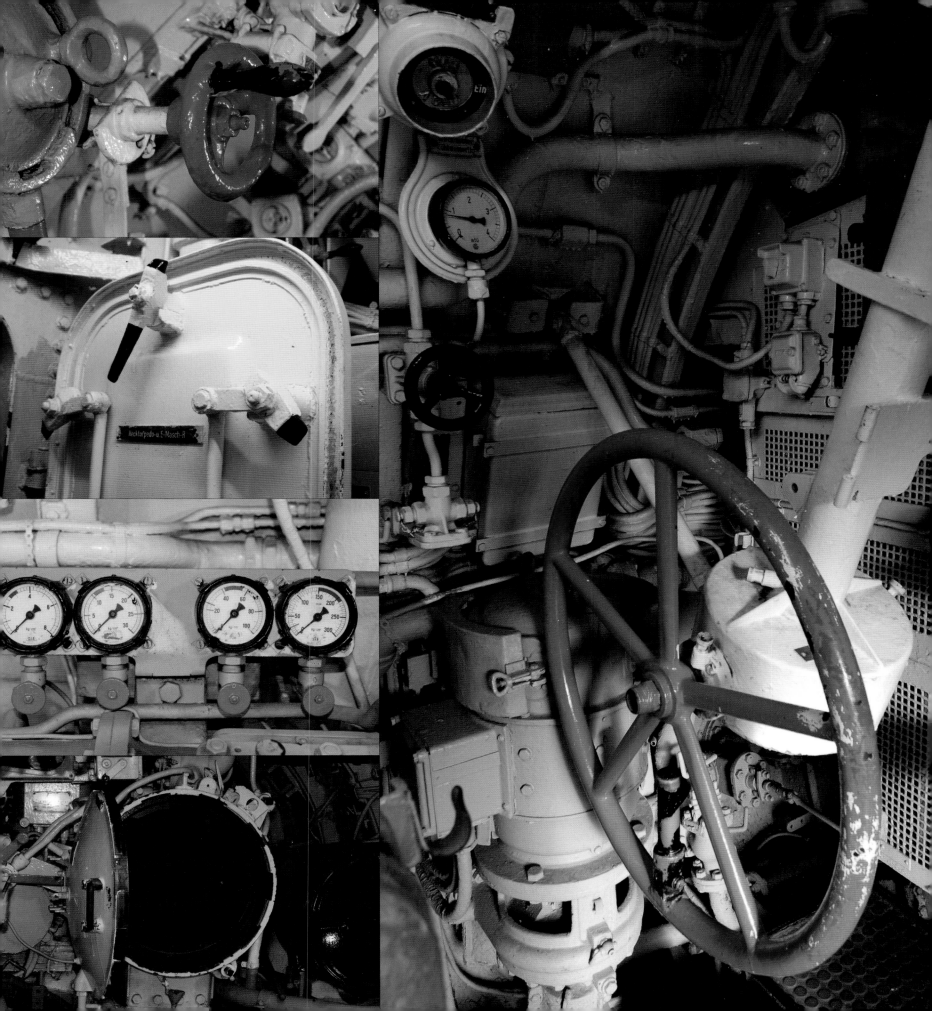

The hunting of U223

The stern torpedo tube of a Type VIIC was often (after September 1943) loaded with a T5 *Zaunkönig* homing torpedo designed to zero in on the high-pitched sound made by military propellers as opposed to the slow rhythmic thump of merchant screws. When enemy destroyers chased *U223* on March 29, 1944, northeast of Palermo in the Mediterranean *Oblt z S* Gerhard Buske was IWO aboard the boat and used the last available chance to deter the attackers.

"We were detected by enemy sonar during the early morning, and several destroyers and smaller gunboats began to hunt us with great determination. We were depth-charged for 25 hours by at least four destroyers. We went down to about 200 to 230m [656 to 755ft], very deep, and the boat creaked and groaned . . . Well, it was very hard with the sound through the water, it was so loud. It was really frightening—it was a hard thing being depth-charged for so long. The air was thick and nearly unbreathable. We were all frightened and tried to will them to go

crew were losing consciousness and our captain, Peter Gerlach, realized that we had to surface and try to escape. We slowly surfaced with the little air left in our tanks and immediately threw open the hatches to get some fresh air. We got the diesels going, but they must have picked us up on radar as the four destroyers opened fire and began to chase us.

"We needed to shake them off, so I ordered the single stern tube with its T5 *Zaunkönig* to be fired. The men set it loose and it headed straight for HMS *Laforey*, which it hit. The ship exploded—we must have hit the magazine— and afterward I learned that there were 189 men killed and only 69 survivors.

Above, left to far right: *The development of the depth charge in World War I, and its subsequent refinement during World War II, gave surface forces their most effective anti-submarine weapon. In 1943 TNT was replaced by Torpex (which was 50 per cent more powerful) as the explosive charge.*

Tauchvorschrift für Mannschaftsdeck
Auf geschlossene Stellung prüfen :

1) Torpedoluk mit Sicherungsklammern u. Verstärkungen
2) Tankseitenv und Zwischenv zum Ausbl Tauchz 5
3) Entlüftung Tauchz 5
4) Bugklappen
5) Seev Torpedoz
6) Lenzv Torpedoz 2 u. 3
7) Peilrohre nach "H" und Torpedoz
8) Bordv für Schmierfettdruckanlage
9) Durchblasev für Seev Torpedoz

auf offene Stellung prüfen :

1) Tankseitenv zum Ausblasen HBT 5
2) Bodenv Hd Luftgr 8
3) Zwischenv Hd Luftgr 8, 7 Stb u. 6 Bb
4) Ventil für Tiefenmesser
5) Ventil für Sauerstoff nach achtern

Above, top: *With fresh water scarce, eau-de-cologne at least helped mask crewmen's body odor. This bottle was recovered from the wreck of U171 near Lorient.*
Left: *"Diving regulations for crew deck"—checklist for the bow room crew to follow prior to diving.*

away; we thought the hull was going to snap and knew that that would be the end of us.

"They launched over 20 separate attacks and chased us around the deep, by which time our air and battery were getting more and more thin. The

"This seemed to make them even more determined to catch us and the captain realized we couldn't escape. He ordered us all out and to abandon ship. The LI, Ernst Scheid, set scuttling charges and was the last man to leave the boat.

I went over the side before the captain, who I think was last to leave. But the boat was circling, still at full speed.

"We were gathering around little rescue boats, many of which were hit as *U223* came back toward us, the propellers chopping the water. So, after she finally went down just over half the crew was rescued and nearly the same number died, most from gunfire. The commander was wounded during the first bombardment and I think maybe they thought another U-boat was there because the *Laforey* had been hit in this position and they dropped more depth charges so that many of those rescued died aboard the ship. We buried them at sea later. At about dawn, with sunrise, we were on and around a little one-man lifeboat, about eight or nine of us. We were near the destroyer that was trying to get the lifeboats on

deck. So I said, 'We will never get this little boat over to them, so anybody who can swim now, just swim—the launch will pick us up and take us to the ship.' So, our *Obersteuermann*, Walter Fitz, and the IIWO, two others, and me, we swam and I told an officer that there were still men out there in the water and he said, 'Oh yes, we won't leave them there,' but I never heard that they were rescued. I know that I heard later on that some men managed to catch ropes from the ship but were pushed down . . . but that's war, you know."

U-boat Prisoners of War

The attrition rate suffered by U-boat men was aggravated—in terms of sheer numbers—by the loss of their fellow seamen through capture. In the early stages of the War captured U-boat men were taken directly to Britain for internment, generally passing through the so-called "London Cage" in Kensington Palace Gardens, London. This was where Britain's "Combined Services Detailed Interrogation Centre" was operated by MI19 from three rather grand houses. (MI19 was the section of the War Office responsible for obtaining information from enemy prisoners of war.) Over the course of the War, the "Cage" developed a formidable, and still controversial, reputation for its unorthodox—and reputedly illegal—interrogation techniques.

Some U-boat prisoners—for example, the officers of *U35*, sunk in 1939—were even held, briefly, in the Tower of London, before being transferred to internment camps outside of the British capital. Canada was for a time the main destination for German PoWs. But when the US entered the conflict in December 1941 the decision was made to accommodate the prisoners there. The German PoWs were transported across the Atlantic aboard merchant ships returning home empty; these were the same convoys the U-boat service was aiming to destroy. Once in the US, PoWs were put to work in factories and farms across the nation.

Generally, the German PoWs were well cared for by their captors. The Allies—unfortunately, but perhaps understandably—mistook fighting ardor and professional pride among Dönitz's men as indications of their commitment to Nazism. As a result, many U-boat PoWs were forced to continue working until long after the end of the War.

Above: Kriegsmarine *identity disc—the* Erkennungsmarke. *These were generally a gold color and bore the wearer's personal identity number and graduating class—in this case, 1942.*

The Homing Torpedo

"The *Zaunkönig*—we called it the 'destroyer-killer.'"—Gerhard Buske, *U223*

By 1944 the Type VIIC U-boat—backbone of Dönitz's fleet—was all but obsolete. The introduction of *Schnorchel*s, radar detectors, increased Flak weaponry, as well as rudimentary radar were all attempts to paper over the cracks highlighted by the design's combat deficiencies in the face of rapid Allied technological advances. Another improvement made by the *Kriegsmarine* was the introduction of more advanced torpedoes. With early faults remedied by 1942, the standard G7a and G7e were fitted with several different modifications to their performance.

The compressed-air-driven G7a was equipped with pattern-running devices, the first known as the "Spring Operated Torpedo" (*Federapparattorpedo*, or FAT), which had a simple guidance system allowing a series of pre-programed long or short legs to be run at right angles to a set length straight run. This in turn was developed into the *Lagenunabhängiger Torpedo* (LUT) that could be fired at any angle and followed a curved path to its target.

Meanwhile the G7e was given more sophisticated modifications. The first passive homing torpedo was developed with the T4 *"Falke"* (falcon), which homed on a simple noise measurement and was intended for use against merchant ships. The T5 that followed was better still. Named the *Zaunkönig* ("wren"), and known to the Allies as the "Gnat," it was for use against convoy escorts, designed to home on propeller cavitation noise of a higher frequency than merchant ships' slow, rhythmic screws. It was first used successfully in combat on September 20, 1943, when the Type VIIC *U270* torpedoed the frigate HMS *Lagan* escorting convoy ON202. The T5 hit the frigate in the stern, killing 28 men and blowing the stern to pieces. Although the ship was later towed to Britain she was declared a total loss.

Dönitz placed great emphasis on this improved weaponry. The first wave of U-boats equipped with the T5 *Zaunkönig* was instructed to keep one loaded in the stern tube as a matter of course. Furthermore Dönitz instructed his captains that:

To begin with, try to make the most of a surprise attack. Do not switch to open attack until the short signal has been received. Then the elimination of the escorting forces must be the main concern. The destruction of a few destroyers will have a demoralizing effect on the enemy and also simplify attacks on the merchant ships.

I expect every commander to make the most of every chance to fire at destroyers. From now on the boat is

Above left: Mechanikermaat *Gerhard Ehlers manhandles the stern torpedo into its tube aboard U564, assisted by Mechanikergefreiter Horst Becker. As in the bow torpedo room, provisions crowd the floor space here.*

Above right: *The tight space in which such physically taxing tasks were performed is evident, as both men work between the greased torpedo and the Junkers air compressor on the boat's starboard side.*

Left: *Commissioning ceremony for a Type VIIC U-boat. The Kriegsmarine's ensign is being run up the boat's small staff, while, on the right, the captain's pennant is streamed for the first time.*

reports were merely the noises of other unrelated explosions. Eventually the Allies developed a noise-generating decoy—the "Foxer"—and the short-lived advantage given to the outdated U-boats was removed.

Above: Bootsmannsmaat Wilhelm Schmitz at work aboard U281. Among Schmitz's tasks as "Seaman Number Three" aboard U281 was the care and maintenance of stored ammunition.

the attacker. Fire first, then submerge to great depth.
After an interval of months, since last May, you will now once again wage submarine war in the North Atlantic, the most important theater. You have been provided with new weapons and gear for this task . . . All the essentials for a successful campaign are to hand. I am sure that you will take up this challenge with the old fighting spirit of the submariner, for this struggle is decisive for our nation's future. The Führer is watching every phase of your struggle. Attack, follow up, sink!
Of course the T5 was not without its flaws, the primary one being that after firing the U-boat had to dive deep, lest the torpedo circle and home in on its firer. Thus the effectiveness could not be observed and frequent success

Left: The stern deck of Type IXC/40 U889. The stern-most gun platform carries a double 37mm Flak weapon, with twin-barreled 20mm guns above it. The two large canisters housed life rafts.

For a breath of air!

Hans Lemke was a 20-year-old "Torpedo Mixer" aboard *U1229* when the Type IXC made its first journey from Norway to the Canadian coast during July and August 1944.

"The journey across the Atlantic was two or three weeks—I can't remember exactly—constantly underwater because of the *Schnorchel*. This wasn't the best of experiences, because when we were in heavy seas the float valve would shut off the *Schnorchel* to stop water coming in. So every time that happened, the diesel still needed air, which it sucked from the inside of the boat.

"It was very boring down there in the torpedo room. I was in charge of the stern section of torpedoes, so I was on my own. All I had to do was make sure that the pressure and all of the other stuff was kept up. I had no other job—I had to be at the ready all the time in case we had to fire.

"We had to sleep down there as well, on bunks fixed between two rails. You would spend your time polishing or checking something—waiting, reading, sleeping, talking. There were about ten of us down there, in a

Both below: *Emergency breathing gear with, left, men in the stern compartment of U79 in the Mediterranean, the emergency helm ready for use.*

Right: *A Type IX U-boat under air attack. As the War progressed, Allied aircraft would become the chief threat to the U-boats in the Atlantic.*

space measuring about 3 x 9m [10 x 30ft]. Some of them, the ordinary seamen, would go up on to the bridge to do their watch, and when they came back down they would sleep. Of course, I knew them all—they had gone through the same training with me and so we talked a lot. I never remember us quarreling really. And so, what did we talk about? Well, the usual sort of thing. Wouldn't it be nice to have a woman and that sort of stuff . . . philosophy, crosswords. We talked about what each of us thought about the universe, God and all of that. We were still pretty optimistic then and no one was anti-Nazi.

"We had a ration of about 15 cigarettes a day—no alcohol on a mission like this. I suppose we had to keep a clear head. Except for the captain who, I believe, did have some spirits with him. The food was very basic—all canned stuff—but it wasn't too bad. We didn't make many demands in those days.

"So, on August 20 we were off Newfoundland and for some reason the captain decided he would bring the submarine to the surface. I don't know why he ordered us up, no one could find out because he was later killed—maybe he wanted a breath of fresh air.

Above: *The lowered* Schnorchel *aboard* U995. *Its siting on Type VIICs meant exhaust could, awkwardly obscure periscope vision.*

"We had absolutely no idea that there were ships in the area and that aircraft were engaged against us. As far as I knew, everything was quiet. But as soon as we went up, we had to dive down very fast again. Alarm!

"I don't think we had dived down 3m [10ft] when a bomb hit us. A lot of damage was done. After about 20 minutes to half an hour we couldn't hold ourselves any longer—we had to surface. Before we even got to the top they started to shoot. But we had to go up and the captain shouted, 'Everyone overboard! Save yourselves!' I was the furthest back so I was the last one to the conning tower. When I came out, I saw them all dead on the deck. Nine aircraft were strafing us.

"I dived straight into the water and I didn't come up until I was yards away. I was in the water for about four hours. I didn't even have a life jacket on—in fact, we had stripped off completely to make us as light as possible. The aircraft kept firing and quite a few of us got shot in the water. There was no need for that because it was

quite obvious that we had abandoned ship. I've never forgiven them for that."

Aboard *U219 Oblt z S* Hans-Joachim Krug endured a forced submersion of 69 hours while escaping enemy attack. During this period the air quality became a primary concern for the well-being of the crew and also their ability to remain below the surface and shake off tenacious pursuit. With systems closed down, the boat drifted between different salinity layers.

"By the end of the time that we had been forced to spend underwater, all CO_2 breathing gear and three quarters of our oxygen stored in pressure bottles had been used up. We were able to check the CO_2 content in the air and it was ten times what it should be. The air inside the boat had gotten so bad that we had to first evacuate the lower deck, then lower bunks, then to even put our heads inside lockers for about two hours each! We had put crew in the unused diesel compartment as the boat floated silently.

"The quality of the air had a direct influence on the crew and how they could function. Even normally, when we were on the surface the only hatches generally open at sea were those in the conning tower—air still needed to be pumped to the boat's extremities. This distribution of fresh clean air was handled by a ventilation system operated from the control room by the *Zentralemaat*. Dräger, the same firm who designed our *Tauchretter* escape gear, constructed a central CO_2 scrubber device that consisted of four metal cartridges in the control room that were connected to the ventilation trunking. We were also able to renew oxygen from storage bottles that could be leaked into the bow, stern, and control rooms. In emergency situations, we of course had breathing gear as well.

"After being down for so long you could see the air. It was foul and barely breathable. Men were listless and unable to do much of anything without collapsing in a heap. It was horrible, but still, it kept us alive. Eventually, we surfaced into a sand storm and were able to escape. When the hatch was opened a column of brown stinking air gushed out and everybody's lungs burned with fresh sea air that was pumped straight away throughout the boat. Those of us lucky enough to go on the tower were overjoyed—even amid all of that sand!"

Above: *A* CO_2 *"scrubbing" cartridge aboard* U995—*vital for ventilation and thus survival during prolonged submergence.*

Above: *One of* U995's *small lockers for enlisted men's personal possessions, located in the bow compartment.*

Rest and Recreation

During the greater part of the War the end of a patrol was marked by cheering crowds, who would greet their returning heroes at the dockside. If at all possible Dönitz would make the effort to welcome each boat home, particularly when he was stationed at Kernevel, opposite the Lorient U-boat pens in France. Often huge numbers of off-duty military personnel from all services, accompanied by flotilla officers and nurses, would be on hand to meet the returning crews, delivering mail, fruit, and drinks to the men once they had been dismissed from a brief parade on deck. After weeks at sea some time was often spent regaining "land legs"—photographs of nurses strolling off the U-boat, arm-in-arm with the crewmen, often mask the fact that the rubber-kneed sailors were being given a helping hand.

After reaching dry land, the crew would sometimes make their way directly to their flotilla headquarters for a brief celebratory meal and drinks. However, the effect of too much alcohol on the men's bodies after weeks at sea could be devastating, and many officers preached

B. d. U. - Zug
Berechtigungskarte
für den _3/4. 10._ 1942
Rückfahrt am _12.10._ 1942
Kommando
Dienststelle Feldpostnummer M 42831

Previous page: Celebrations began almost as soon as a safely returned U-boat had docked.
Left: A very rare example of a ticket for the BdU train, issued to Stabsobermaschinist Alfons Grünhäuser.

moderation, at least until they had cleaned themselves up and eaten. The returning crew would collect their stored seabags before being transported to barracks for the unmitigated joy of a warm shower and the chance to wash off weeks' worth of accumulated grime. Generally, the first port of call after this would be the nearest *U-Bootsheim*, a recreation center specifically reserved for the use of U-boat men. Here, they could drink, watch movies, or play games. They would also be eligible to collect whatever back-pay had accrued during their time at sea, before venturing forth to spend it.

As soon as was practicable, the U-boat commander would meet with Dönitz for a personal debriefing so that his Chief of Operations could collect the necessary facts about the particular patrol. An experienced submariner himself, Dönitz was able to develop a "feel" for the course his strategy was taking at sea from these debriefings. He was equally free with his praise as

Above: The band strikes up as Günther Prien brings his U47 into St Nazaire; Prien's "Snorting Bull" emblem can just be seen on the conning tower.

Above: A typical welcome reception for a returning U-boat—nurses, off-duty military personnel, and the very few civilians allowed into the military dock area.

Far right: *The sun-lamp room was one of the facilities available to men of the 3rd U-Flotilla based in La Pallice. These bearded submariners, recently returned from patrol, may have seen hardly any natural sunlight while at sea.*

Above: Kptlt *Heinrich Timm and his crew of U251 are welcomed home in 1943.*

Below: *The entrance to the special underground "hotel" built for U-boat personnel in Lorient, France. Efforts have been made to render what was essentially a concrete bunker as welcoming as possible.*

with his criticism, though if he judged a commander to have fallen short of his expectations that man could be relieved of his command immediately. (He also often asked other officers and men what had gone on, and came to a number of wrong conclusions as a result.) At this time a list of those who would be awarded medals would also be drawn up by the commander, in consultation with his senior men. The list would ultimately be passed to BdU, who would authorize the granting of decorations. (Many medals, however, were awarded the moment the boat put into port.)

Between patrols, if possible, U-boat crews were generally given home leave in strict rotation. The *Kriegsmarine* organized a special train service for them that ran from occupied France to Germany, known to the U-boat men as the BdU train (*BdU Zug*). The existence of the train eventually became known to the Allies and they became a favored target for fighter-bombers. In time, many trains were fitted with Flak guns for protection, but they ceased operation altogether in 1944.

Ashore in occupied countries, crews were billeted in the port town itself at first, before these became frequent targets for the Allied bombers. Subsequently, as well as the heavily reinforced bunkers that were built to shelter the crews alongside those covering their boats in harbor, camps were established in the surrounding countryside.

In France the *Wehrmacht* requisitioned hundreds of châteaus of varying sizes for the use of their troops, and U-boat men were no exception. Generally staffed with French workers they were often palatial and remote, allowing men to unwind in a state of luxury that was often no longer attainable in Germany itself. While relations with the local populations in the occupied countries were generally better than has often been reported by historians, various accounts have also pointed to the worsening of this fragile relationship as Germany's fortunes waned. Many of the port cities became more dangerous and men on leave were generally

instructed to travel in small groups lest they be targeted by the French Resistance.

As the War progressed, men traveling home to Germany were allowed to take as much food and other goods as they liked with them—for many items were becoming scarce in the homeland. In Germany, cities and towns who "adopted" a particular U-boat frequently hosted entire crews, or at least those who were available for leave. Dönitz also organized special holidays in the German and Austrian mountains where the men could learn to ski under the instruction of trained *Gebirgsjäger* (mountain troops). Even here they were subject to special attention by the propaganda service, who would take care to portray the high standards of care given to the U-boat men, so as to promote the service to those who were considering enlisting in this "elite" branch of the *Kriegsmarine*.

Hans-Rudolf Rösing held the Staff position of FdU West for much of the War, based at first in Angers, France, and then briefly in Norway. Part of his job was to ensure the well-being of the men, including their off-duty recreational needs: "I went to the flotillas whenever I had the opportunity, and of course I also kept close contact with the commanders. And each of them came to Angers to report when they came back from a mission. They then went to Berlin and reported directly to Dönitz. Those reports sometimes took hours, as Dönitz was very eager to get a thorough picture of every action and all of the conditions experienced by his commanders. We even had a special BdU train that was for the exclusive use of U-boat crews to travel between the bases in western France and Paris, and then on to Germany.

"Though Dönitz took great interest in his men's welfare I only saw Hitler once at a U-boat base. It was the early weeks of the War and he came to Wilhelmshaven to see Otto Schuhart and his crew from *U29*, who had just sunk HMS *Courageous*. There he met the crew and then went into the officers' mess, where many of the flotilla commanders sat around a table with him. I wanted to see a little bit more of Hitler and so I followed and was standing beside him as he spoke to everybody. That was the one time I was up close to him and I looked into his eyes and there was nothing. I remember it clearly; they were cold and empty, almost too big. It was very odd. But he had no real understanding of naval warfare anyway.

"I was promoted to the post of FdU by Dönitz after my combat patrols on *U48*. My office in France was responsible for many aspects of the logistical war. For example, we had the journalists of the *Propaganda Kompanie* attached to my staff and we allocated them to

Above: *Dönitz (far left) and Rösing with the pet donkey at FdU West headquarters, Angers. Rösing's staff hockey team was named the "Donkey's Eleven" in the animal's honor.*

boats once BdU decided they should go to sea. One of them was Lothar-Günther Buchheim, who later wrote *Das Boot*. I actually quite liked him when I met him during the War. He was an excellent artist and an intelligent man.

"A most important task for the FdU was acquiring buildings for the men to relax in between patrols. I also did the same for a period for the Italian boats stationed in

Bordeaux, but their Admiral did not want his men stationed anywhere too quiet—they wanted to be in the town, with all its action! I also had the visiting Japanese crews to look after, and we took them to our châteaus and arranged girls for them, and so on. The only thing they were particularly sensitive about was their tea; they had to bring their own with them. It was interesting, actually, because we Europeans thought the Japanese had no fear of death—kamikaze and so on—but after being around them in social situations we realized they were as scared of death as we were.

"In some ways I was not popular with some of the combat crews. They didn't know what I and my staff were doing as they got their operational details directly from BdU. And, later in the War in France, I made it my job to keep men busy with sports and so forth, and sometimes they may not have really wanted to! In Angers we had a hockey team called the 'Donkey's Eleven' because we had a donkey in our backyard as a pet. In this team I played Left Back, but of course only when we had the time!"

Ironically it was not only the *Kriegsmarine* who paid such close attention to the rest and recreation habits of the U-boat service. Lieutenant Angus MacLean Thuermer was an American Naval Intelligence officer attached to 30 Assault Unit, Royal Marines, whose sole mission was to

Above: *U-boat men relaxing and playing games; they are clearly very young—a reminder that the majority were either teenagers or in their early 20s.*
Below: *A U-boat technician relaxing with a Luftwaffe auxiliary worker. Among his awards is the "Spanish Cross," indicating that he is a veteran of the Spanish Civil War.*

gather intelligence on the German navy, particularly its U-boat men. "In quizzing U-boat prisoners, US Naval Intelligence took advantage of the German naval medical corps' concerns with the submariners' health. Their doctors were particularly concerned with checking and treating venereal disease, which broke out among the crews while on war patrols. One method of trying to control the disease was the practice of issuing a card to each sailor who visited a bordello in the French ports where the *Kriegsmarine* had bases. Each time a sailor visited a *Wehrmacht* bordello he got a card that named the port, the house, his partner, and the date. The sailor would take these cards on war patrols. If the man came down with what seemed like venereal disease, the U-boat medics would radio back to the base the names and dates of all the contacts on the cards in the sailor's pockets. Presumably the women would then be medically inspected and treated, or put out of the harlot business.

"When a U-boat was blasted to the surface in the course of a fight and depth charging, many of the sailors had hip pockets full of these cards. There it was: names of partners and dates, and the name of the port and bordello. Indeed from the size of some of the packets of cards some sailors had with them, they had little time to take tourist tours to French cathedrals!

"When it was time to interrogate the men, if they remembered the cards at all, they had usually forgotten that they were taken away from them with all their wet uniforms when they were sailing back to an Allied port. It

would be established, sometimes even while they were being brought back, that the U-boat came, for instance, from the 1st U-Flotilla pens at Brest. Then, advantage could be taken of all the intelligence that had been acquired from all German Armed Forces Houses of Prostitution cards. We came to know which tart was working at what house in what navy port. Most of our "slut"

statistics came from the U-boat medical cards plus subsequent interrogations. Our precise information about this was casually delivered by interrogators in an offhand, small-talk sort of way. It might go something like this:

"'Ah . . . I understand that your boat *U764* was based in Brest?'

"'I'm not allowed to say, Sir.'

"'Oh yes, alright. Not important . . . just making some small talk while we're getting these details down. Well, in any case, you won't be seeing any more of those French ladies at the *Café des Trois Soeurs* will you, mate? Sorry about that!' Hearty chuckle by the interrogator as he shuffles his papers.

"'Café what, Sir?'

"'Oh come on now, mate—don't say that! You don't know the *Café des Trois Soeurs*, or as you U-boat men call it, *Café Six-Tits*? Our own men couldn't pick a better name . . . and Jeanne Marie? Still in business?' Of course all the time the interrogator knew that the man sitting across from him had been one of her partners. You know that from reading the cards that had been in his pocket. It gave most of the prisoners being interrogated the impression that if the Allied intelligence knew the most intimate details of their shore leave, they probably knew everything. So this 'everything' might as well include a question about a triggering device on a torpedo. It was just something else that the interrogating officer needed to 'fill out his form.'"

Below: *The main entrance to the casino at La Baule, six miles (10km) west of St Nazaire. A thriving tourist destination in prewar France, this building was opened in 1904 and served as the warrant officer's mess for the 6th and 7th U-Flotillas during World War II.*

Below: *Karl Dönitz and some of his BdU staff relaxing on the terrace at Kernevel, opposite Lorient's U-boat base.*

Propaganda

The U-boat service had attracted the attention of Germany's highly effective propaganda service right from the outbreak of hostilities in September 1939. Several of the early commanders became celebrities in Germany. For example, after *U47* penetrated Scapa Flow and sunk HMS *Royal Oak* in October, 1939, Günther Prien and his entire crew were flown to Berlin, where they were driven to the Reich Chancellery along streets lined with cheering crowds.

Propaganda service reporters were also frequent visitors aboard combat U-boats, using still and movie cameras to record the activities of Dönitz's vaunted "Grey Wolves." The reporters were not adverse to some trickery as, among the staged shots that littered newsreel films were some "special effects" provided by the Ufa Film Studios, which were directly controlled by Propaganda Minister Joseph Goebbels. The most famous example of this followed the beginning of "Operation Paukenschlag"—the U-boat assault on the United States immediately following the December, 1941 declaration of war. In reality, Reinhard Hardegen's *U123* came sufficiently close to New York City to be able to see the glow of its lights in the sky. In the newsreel report, however, German cinema audiences were bedazzled with vivid shots of the Manhattan skyline, courtesy of Ufa.

On a more prosaic level, some of the most famous photographs made aboard U-boats were snapped through the periscope by means of a specially adapted camera fitting. Erich Topp, Captain of the "Red Devil" boat, *U552*, remembered such photographs being made: "We sometimes 'entertained' guests from the Propaganda Service. My U-boat, for instance, had a Leica camera installed that operated even when we were diving. So, diving and surfacing was filmed on this camera, which was operated from the control room. I also once took a cameraman to sea. Kiefer was his name, and he took many pictures and some film, most of which are quite well known now. They show such things as the control room during a submerged attack, and my officers and I on our bridge. On this trip we took part in a convoy battle during which we hit a tanker that exploded, so he had much to film. He was a man of the *Propaganda Kompanie*, not a sailor. He had only the role of cameraman, no other assigned duties. But this was really only an occasional event, having a reporter or cameraman on board. We once had another reporter on board and he recorded everything that happened. During one attack he was talking throughout, and it was very dramatic—we were chased by a destroyer, hitting merchant ships and so on, and he was speaking, speaking, all the time. I have it on record now.

"There were many staged shots taken, some of it is now famous with me attacking merchant shipping using the navigation scope . . . Men handled such exposure differently. Some, like 'Teddy' Suhren were reluctant to enter the

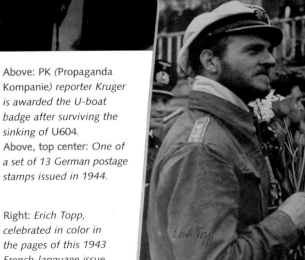

Above: *PK (Propaganda Kompanie) reporter Kruger is awarded the U-boat badge after surviving the sinking of U604.*
Above, top center: *One of a set of 13 German postage stamps issued in 1944.*

Right: *Erich Topp, celebrated in color in the pages of this 1943 French-language issue of Signal magazine.*

Die Wehrmacht

HERAUSGEGEBEN VOM OBERKOMMANDO DER WEHRMACHT

Weihnachten, durch das Luk eines U-Boots gesehen: Die Feier der Freiw

Die Kriegsmarine

Jugend aufs Meer!

U-Boot auf der Fahrt ins Operationsgebiet im Schwarzen Meer

Left: Two of the most popular military propaganda periodicals. The December 1939 issue of Die Wehrmacht *leads with "Christmas seen through a U-boat's hatch," while the 1943 issue of* Die Kriegsmarine *shows an artist's view of a U-boat in service in the Black Sea.*

Below: Günther Prien's crew of U47 leaving the Reichs Chancellory after an audience with Hitler. They had successfully breached the defenses of Scapa Flow and sunk HMS Royal Oak.

spotlight, while others enjoyed their fame. You could often drink and eat for free in Germany if you were recognized!"

Ironically, much of the propaganda about the U-boat service is still widely believed, many years after the end of the War. One example is the so-called "Happy Time," the period in 1940 when U-boats were perceived to rule the waves. Jurgen Oesten survived the War after captaining three separate U-boats and holding several staff positions during those tumultuous years. He entered combat as captain of the Type IIC *U61* and ended the War aboard the Type IXD2 *U861*—the last U-boat to successfully return from the Far East to Norway. He hadn't at the time, and still did not as of November 2006, hold any illusions about the reality of Dönitz's U-boat war: "I think it was in 1938 that we had some sort of war game, trying to establish how many submarines would be necessary to cut the supply line to Britain that stretched across the Atlantic. The conclusion was that at the beginning of any war we needed 300 boats in service at our disposal in the Atlantic . . . With this number of boats it might have been possible to cut the supply lines within two years, effectively. I think at the beginning of the War we had some 60

U-boats; only 40 or so of them were combat vessels and 20 of them were too small for such a vast ocean. So, it was quite clear to us all that our chances were less than limited. In addition, we had been working with a rate of more than 50 per cent losses right from the beginning. The so-called 'Happy Time' is a myth. There were too many plaques on walls remembering fallen comrades right from the War's beginning.

"We were not at all prepared for this sort of fight, but Hitler was too stupid. He thought he could play around in Europe without Britain's interference. Dönitz was a good naval officer and because of that his U-boat war was carried right through to the bitter end. His handicap was that he could be influenced by emotions and Hitler was able to let him swim in a soup of emotions, disregarding the actual facts. I think, looking back, we managed to cut about 1 per cent of the supplies to Britain. It was never a 'Happy Time.'"

Kptlt Jurgen Oesten was tasked in 1942 with establishing a new U-boat flotilla in the French port of Brest. Coupled with his military responsibilities he had to consider the needs of his men and staff: "When I was tasked with setting up the 9th U-Flotilla in Brest there was no space as the installations that had been used by the French Navy, such as the magnificent naval officers' school atop the hill, had all been requisitioned by the 1st U-Flotilla. I found a raw building—an unfinished hospital on which work had stopped at the beginning of the War. I tracked down the two young architects in Paris and managed to agree with them that, yes, the War was deeply unpleasant, but managed to convince them to help in finishing the building using the workforce of the Organization Todt.

"One night I was drinking with the local chief of the Organization Todt when he told me that he was being replaced by another man, and asked whether I wanted a nice château for billeting my men. He said that he would pass it on to me rather than his replacement. So, at 6am we drove out to Logonna, which had been refitted by the Todt workers. I ended up staying there for about half a year and had a very good contact with its owner, a Marquis who had other châteaus in France as well. The Marquis had employed an English nurse to look after his kids, and the Germans had interned her. I managed to get her out and back to him. I also took care of the local villagers by preventing the requisitioning of their horses by the *Wehrmacht*."

Later, Oesten became commander of *U861*, that reached Penang on September 23, 1944. Once there he coordinated with the local German command to provide areas for his crew to recharge their batteries before work began on overhauling their boat:

Above: A Bootsmannsmaat's dress jacket, the red trade badge denoting a qualified Flak artillery leader.
Left: Officers of the 2nd U-Flotilla relaxing at the "Moulin de Kersalo" in Lager Lemp near Lorient. The requisitioned mill still stands amidst the remains of the camp.

"When in the Far East we were billeted in conditions that had nearly been forgotten in Germany. There were beautiful buildings in the town near the docks as well as rest areas in the hills, where the temperatures were not so high. The houses up there had actually been built for that reason for the European colonial residents before the War, and we were happy to use them. Each house had a small number of staff who looked after the men. However, relations with the Japanese were often strained as they had established a kind of racial war against the white man—which, of course, we were! In fact we were the only white people running around free. This caused problems, at least on a few occasions. When my crew saw British

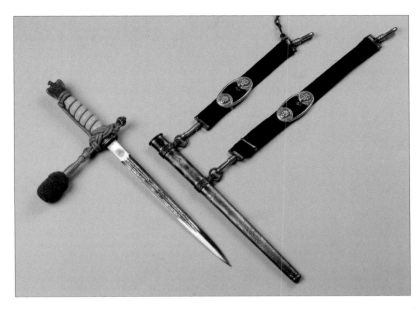

Above: Kriegsmarine *officer's dagger with standard-issue hangers and woven silver aluminum cord, known as a "Portepee." It was worn with dress uniform.*

prisoners being taken to work by the Japanese they gave them cigarettes and so on, which the guards didn't like. One of my men was sitting at a bar in Singapore when he was approached by a Japanese soldier, who started shouting at him as he thought he might be British. But the sailor was faster than him and threw him in the water! Later, there were apologies and the matter was closed. But there was always a lingering mistrust between us. We had no Japanese workers on our boats and vice-versa, we always looked after such things ourselves. However, I, for example, had a very good contact with the liaison officer assigned to me by the Japanese Navy.

"One of the other problems with the Japanese was that they couldn't drink very much, so our boys always had to have a second party to go to. The Japanese would get so drunk they fell asleep early on, so we used to pick them up and put them in storage somewhere before carrying on with somebody else, the boys with their girls and so on. You know, when we got to Penang I went to the Japanese Admiral and said, 'I would like a hotel,' and we were given the Shanghai Hotel that had been requisitioned. I had a crew of youngsters who were born in the 1920s, and of course it was their first time in the tropics or abroad and I didn't want any of them to get any venereal disease, so we started up this hotel and hired nice girls who were checked by our medical officer. We made contracts with these girls that if they only wanted to dance then that was okay and they were given a certain color of flower to wear, but if they were willing to sleep with the boys then they wore another type of flower. And we arranged with them that while they were under contract with us they had to stay at the hotel, so they could get no diseases elsewhere. So, by taking this precaution, none of my crew picked up venereal disease. There were other boats that had two months in Jakarta or Batavia and half the boat had syphilis after going into the back-street Chinese houses. I arranged with my boys not to go into the Chinese quarters, but to stay at the Shanghai Hotel.

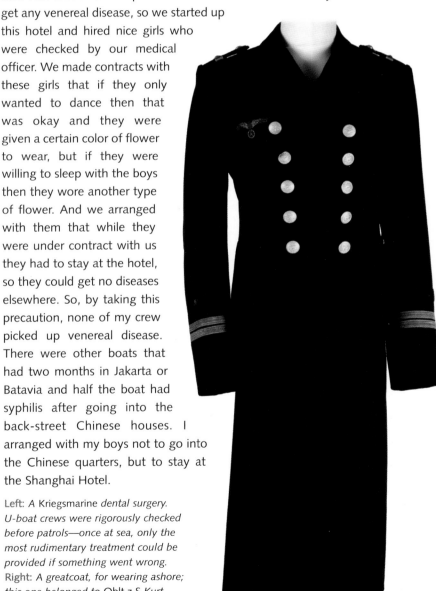

Left: *A Kriegsmarine* dental surgery. *U-boat crews were rigorously checked before patrols—once at sea, only the most rudimentary treatment could be provided if something went wrong.*
Right: *A greatcoat, for wearing ashore; this one belonged to Oblt z S Kurt Brückner of U502.*

"Because, you know, two years before the War I was Watch Officer on *U20* and at that time, during years of peace, we had had the time to be properly and thoroughly trained. After spending so much time together we were able to send men from the diesel room onto the bridge—everybody knew what to do. Then of course I got my own boat during the War, another little one, the *U61*. Then I moved on to the Type IX *U106*, in which I damaged the old battlewagon HMS *Malaya*. Years later I met a man off

Above: *A banquet organized for the returning crew of a combat U-boat. After a prolonged period at sea, with no (or very limited) access to alcohol or rich food, the men had to exercise some caution, in case their systems became overloaded. So it was not uncommon for nurses to be on hand.*

that ship and he was grateful because he and his mates spent three-quarters of a year in a New York shipyard and had the time of their lives! But anyway, it was all this experience of handling crews that gave me the insight to provide my men with the proper rest and recreation facilities. It takes about a year to know a man inside and out, and then you can make the best use of his abilities. There were also ways to handle the men aboard the boat. The doctor onboard, together with the wireless people, made a weekly newspaper to keep spirits high during the voyage and give involvement for men when at sea.

"It was common knowledge, of course, that in the transfer of U-boat personnel between boats there was no

comradeship at all because we all tried to get people who had been on the boat before back, because you knew them. The same went for the crews, too, who wanted to remain in the boat with a commander that they knew. I had a man, for example—Berthold Wendelmuth—who had been an ordinary sailor on *U61*, an *Obersteuermann* on *U106*, and then on *U861*. I wanted to have him awarded the 'Collar Iron' [Knight's Cross] and recommended so on May 2, 1945, but I got no reaction to my suggestion. He had certainly earned the award and I would have liked him to have had it, but apparently it didn't work like that anymore. Also, for instance the IIWO on that last boat had been *Funkmaat* on *U61*. I found him after they had made him an officer and I wanted him back."

In France several requisitioned châteaus were placed at the disposal of U-boat personnel between patrols. While some men would return to vacation in Germany, others would unwind in palatial surroundings with a staff on hand to cater for their every need. Paul Helmchen was in the crew of the ill-fated *U441*, based at Brest as part of the 1st U-Flotilla: "I was on the Flak-trap *U441* when we sailed with the increased weaponry during two patrols. My station was in the engine room. I was aboard when we were badly damaged and lost some men, but we also managed to hit the enemy aircraft. After these patrols we lived in Brest, in the old French Navy base. But we could also go to the *U-Bootwiesen*, the so-called 'pastures.' There, we could really unwind. The one I remember was near Châteauneuf de Faou in a château called *Trévarez*, built in the late 19th and early 20th century by a Marquis. It was a beautiful red building with extensive grounds in which you could forget the depth charges and air attacks. Some men brought their 'wives' with them to the building and we were very well looked after. Ironically, it became a target for the RAF, who bombed it, after which men had to stay in town. But I had left by then. I became chief engineer aboard *U1407*, the 'Walther boat,' that ran on hydrogen peroxide and was supposed to revolutionize the War. Needless to say, it didn't work in the end."

If not billeted at remote buildings, men at rest could also stay in specially constructed camps, such as "Lager Lemp" situated outside Lorient. Construction had begun before Allied air raids hit their peak in 1943. Situated off the main road between Pont Scorff and Caudan, the camp stood in the wooded grounds of Moulin Kersalo, a

requisitioned lakeside mill. The lake, surrounded by a solid walkway and used by relaxing submariners for swimming and boating, was eventually camouflaged to prevent the RAF targeting (the RAF knew the camp's location thanks to the French Resistance). Hans Goebeler of the 2nd U-Flotilla's *U505* remem-

bered the "hidden camp": "We had a so-called *U-bootsheim* in Lorient, where they showed the latest German films, and where we could basically amuse ourselves playing cards, writing, and sending letters or enjoying the cheap beer. Of course that was never enough, and sooner or later we would wander off to the civilian parts and find ladies with whom we could enjoy a dance or two, or more . . .

"Eventually, once the bombers began to pay too much attention to Lorient we and the men of the 10th U-Flotilla were quartered at Lager Lemp. Now this was a less than satisfactory affair as there was only one small town nearby—Pont Scorff—and fewer ladies to go around between us U-boat men and the *Wehrmacht* infantry, who were also stationed in that area. There were plenty of fights at first, although over time this changed, and we would actually invite our new friends to enjoy some of the benefits of U-boat canteens in the Lorient *U-bootsheim*. Eventually, the gates at Lager Lemp began to get crowded with French girls and vendors, which of course meant that the camp was soon going to be pinpointed by the Allied bombers as well. We only had shallow slit trenches there—these were handy for crawling under the wire for illicit rendezvous, but [their shallowness] meant that air attacks would probably be deadly. [Those in charge of the camp] even went as far as draping camouflage netting over conspicuous features, even the lake!"

Top right: The main entrance to Lager Lemp near Lorient. As with many barracks, it was named for a fallen hero of the U-boat service.
Center right and lower right: Inside Lager Lemp was a small lake, where the men could swim or go boating. The lake was later draped with camouflage netting in an attempt to conceal the camp's location from Allied reconnaissance aircraft.

Far right, above: Kptlts *Rolf Mützelburg* (left) and *Adalbert Schnee* are presented with Oak Leaves to their Knight's Crosses on August 8, 1942. Mützelburg was killed in an accident at sea a little over a month later.

Below: *Skiing in Bavaria was popular with U-boat crews on leave, especially those with a Patenschaft (twinning) arrangement with a local town.*

It was common practice for German cities and towns to "adopt" a U-boat, under what was called the *Patenschaft* system. Often the crews would be hosted at their sponsoring town by the local people, as Wolfgang Schiller of *U505* remembered: "Our sponsor town was Bad Wiessee on Bavaria's Tegernsee. That's a little town mainly used for skiers and people to go for relaxation. A very nice town with a lake and everything that goes with it, with beautiful hotels, and we were invited there right after the voyage in which *U505* had been badly bombed. I participated in this vacation where we stayed at the Hotel Wolf, which had been specially reserved for U-boat

Far right, below: *A Patenschaft certificate between U562 and the Rhine city of Neuss, which had "adopted" its crew.*

personnel, and then the Bavarians saw for the first time the 'Navy on Skis.' Of course for us it was an experience, and we were young people, and we were also able to pull a few things off in that town so that the folks were always amused by us, right. And we—I also have the picture with

me—we were invited by another town that was in the area to a celebration—and there, our submarine crew was photographed with the Party bigwigs."

Erich Topp recalled spending time between patrols, both in Paris and once even at Hitler's mountain retreat in Bavaria: "The Scherezade was in Paris; it was very popular. It was run by Russians—they had left their own country when the Bolsheviks took control. It was our second home there. Everybody had somebody there, with whom he was very much in love. At one point my very good friend Endrass and I invited two of our lady friends from the Scherezade crew to our villa in La Baule, near St Nazaire, and we lived there together for a while. He had the Belgian Monique and I was with a Russian dancer Patti Bearse. It was a wonderful part of our lives. She was the daughter of the Russian General, Aristov. I wanted to marry her, but when I asked her, in 1942, her mother was living with her in Paris. She said, 'Well, this is going to be a long war and I have to look after my mother. So what will happen to us when the War ends, and we are still friends with the Germans? It makes no sense and I have to survive.' So she went the other way, later made contact with the Americans, and married one of them.

"Until 1943 it was mainly volunteers who wanted to join the U-boats because they had the greatest publicity at that time. We had recreation centers in Austria and other parts of the country, and so we were treated very well . . . Once I was even a guest at Berchtesgaden [Hitler's retreat in the German Alps] where the 'greats' of our leadership stayed. You see, Martin Bormann's wife was the sister of my crew member, Walter Buch, who was in turn the son of the Nazi Party's highest-ranking lawyer. I had been with Hitler twice at his Wolfschanze headquarters and once in Vilnisia, so I had met Bormann several times. One day we were talking and he said, 'You know, my wife and I would be happy if you would pay us a visit at Pullach.' So I did, and met his eight children. One of his daughters later became my goddaughter and she married an Italian doctor, but she died while giving birth. Anyway, I had a good contact with the Bormann family, and after Pullach we went to Obersaltzberg, where there was the 'Platterhof'—a hotel—in which I was invited to stay for 14 days, together with Teddy Suhren. So, we were both in the privileged position of being guests of the Party at the Platterhof. We were free to do as we pleased—no restrictions or anything—and we were very happy as it is a truly beautiful area.

"One day Bormann invited us to the Eagle's Nest and there we saw the wonderfully shaped house that he had built as a present for Hitler. We sat at a table and I was beside a young lady. Hitler's doctor was there and we were drinking coffee. I was talking to the young lady and asked, 'What are you doing here?' and she said, 'I am a secretary,' and Teddy kept kicking me under the table to say 'Shut up!'. He knew more than me. Of course it was Eva Braun and I later found out who she was. But I must say she was very nice and open, and so we invited her the next day to be our guest—of course not in the hotel, but in another house that she came to. Teddy was quite different to me. I was always quite reserved, but Teddy—well, he was very outgoing and after [drinking] a little alcohol and so on, Eva Braun became very open too, complaining that she was always put aside when official guests visited Hitler and she was unable to become his wife and represent him. She was unhappy about that. Teddy of course was offering any help that he could. Teddy was a master of these kinds of conversations!"

Above and left (from left): A presentation version of the Iron Cross Second Class; War Merit Cross with Swords, awarded for exceptional service in the front line (though not in action); Wehrmacht four-year service award; the "Anschluss" medal commemorating participation in the annexation of Austria in 1938.

Glossary

Aale German for "eels;" German naval slang for torpedoes.

Abwehr The name of the German Intelligence Service.

Arzt German for doctor.

ASDIC Term applied to the sonar equipment used for locating submerged submarines. A powerful and effective weapon, it emitted a distinct "ping" when locating the target. The word ASDIC is an acronym for "Anti-Submarine Detection Committee," the organization that began research into this device in 1917.

B.d.U. (Befehlshaber der Unterseeboote) U-boat High Command.

Bold The abbreviation of the German word *Kobold*, or goblin; it was used to describe an acoustic decoy, known also as the "submarine bubble target," that comprised a small cylindrical mesh container filled with calcium hydride. When ejected from a submerged U-boat, the compound reacted with seawater to give off hydrogen bubbles, and thus a false echo to ASDIC operators. It was simple but effective.

Enigma Name for the coding machine used by the German armed forces throughout World War II.

F.d.U. (Führer der Unterseeboote) Regional German U-boat command.

Falke T4 sound homing torpedo, designed to home on the low-pitched sound of merchant ship propellers.

F.A.T. (Federapparat) German T3 pattern-running torpedo.

Flag Officer A general term encompassing naval officers generally of *Konteradmiral* and above who are entitled to fly a personal flag.

Flakfalle A "Flak trap;" specially modified anti-aircraft U-boats.

G7a Standard German air-driven torpedo; known as *Ato*.

G7e Standard German electric torpedo (wakeless); known as *Eto*.

GRT Gross Registered Tonnage (one ton equals 100 cubic feet cargo capacity); a standard way of judging merchant shipping size.

Heer German Army.

Ing. (Ingenieur) German for Engineer. Inserted after rank, e.g. *Leutnant (Ing.)*

KTB (Kriegstagebuch) War Diary. Kept by the commander during a U-boat's patrol. The hand-written version would later be typed up for the official records. Included torpedo-shooting diagrams.

Kameradschaft German veterans' organization; *U-Bootskameradschaft* comprising veterans of Germany's U-boat service.

Kriegsmarine German Navy.

LI (Leitender Ingenieur) Chief Engineer.

Lords *Kriegsmarine* slang for enlisted men.

Luftwaffe German Air Force.

M.A.A. (Marine Artillerie Abteilung) German naval artillery unit.

O.K.M. (Oberkommando der Marine) German Naval Command.

O.K.W. (Oberkommando der Wehrmacht) German Military Forces Command.

Oberfeldwebelraum Chief Petty Officers' Quarters.

Offiziersraum Officers' Quarters.

Organization Todt German labor and construction service named after its creator, **Fritz Todt**. The OT, as it was known, comprised men from all over Europe, including countries that remained steadfastly neutral throughout the conflict, such as Spain.

S-Boot (Schnellboot) German Motor Torpedo Boat.

S.K.L. (Seekriegsleitung) Naval War Staff.

Schnorchel Snorkel; the device which, when raised, allowed fresh air to be drawn into a submerged U-boat, enabling the diesel engines to be run while underwater.

Sonderführer A specially commissioned officer; often a temporary rank held by men such as reporters.

Stab Staff.

Unteroffizierraum Petty Officers' Quarters.

WO (Wachoffizier) Watch Officer. There were three separate U-boat watch crews, each consisting of an officer or senior NCO, Petty Officer, and two ratings. The ship's First Watch Officer (IWO) would be the Executive Officer (second in command), the Second Watch Officer (IIWO) the ship's designated Second Officer, and the Third Watch Officer (IIIWO) often the *Obersteuermann* (Navigation Officer).

Wehrmacht German Armed Forces.

Wintergarten Nickname given to the open-railed extension astern of the conning tower, built to accommodate increased Flak weaponry. Known to the Allies as the "bandstand."

Zaunkönig T5 sound homing torpedo, designed to target the higher pitched propellers of a warship.

Zentrale U-boat central control room.

Zentralemaat Senior Control Room Mate.

Table of comparative ranks

German (Abbreviation)	British/American
Grossadmiral	Admiral of the Fleet/Fleet Admiral
Admiral	Admiral
Vizeadmiral (V.A.)	Vice Admiral
Konteradmiral (K.A.)	Rear Admiral
Kapitän zur See (Kpt.z.S.)	Captain
Fregattenkapitän (F.K.)	Commander
Korvettenkapitän (K.K.)	Commander
Kapitänleutnant (Kptlt.)	Lieutenant Commander
Oberleutnant zur See (Oblt.z.S.)	Lieutenant
Leutnant zur See (L.z.S.)	Sub-Lieutenant/Lieutenant (jg)
Oberfähnrich	Senior Midshipman
Fähnrich	Midshipman
Stabsobersteuermann	Senior Quartermaster/Warrant Quartermaster
Obersteuermann	Quartermaster (also U-boat's Navigation officer)
Obermaschinist	Senior Machinist/Warrant Machinist
Bootsmann	Boatswain
Oberbootsmannsmaat	Boatswain's Mate
Bootsmannsmaat	Coxswain
-Maat (trade inserted as suffix)	Petty Officer
Maschinenobergefreiter	Leading Seaman Machinist
Funkobergefreiter	Leading Seaman Telegraphist
Matrosenobergefreiter	Leading Seaman
Mekanikergefreiter	Able Seaman Torpedo Mechanic
Maschinengefreiter	Able Seaman Mechanic
Matrosengefreiter	Able Seaman
Matrose	Ordinary Seaman

Bibliography

Barnett, Correlli: *Engage The Enemy More Closely* (W.W. Norton & Co, 1991)

Bekker, C.D.: *Swastika at Sea* (William Kimber & Co, 1953)

Blair, Clay: *Hitler's U-Boat War, Volumes 1 & 2* (Cassell, 2000)

Brendon, Piers: *The Dark Valley* (Jonathan Cape, 2000)

Brennecke, Jochen, *The Hunters And The Hunted* (Burke Publishing, 1958)

Busch, Harald: *U-boats At War* (Putnam, 1955)

Churchill, Winston: *The Second World War, Volumes 1 to 6* (Cassell, 1954)

Dönitz, Karl: *Memoirs: Ten Years And Twenty Days* (Greenhill Books, 1990)

Franks, Norman: *Search, Find And Kill* (Grub Street, 1995)

Hague, Arnold: *The Allied Convoy System* (Chatham Publishing, 2000)

Herzog, Bodo: *Deutsche U-Boote 1906–1966* (Karl Müller Verlag, 1996)

Hess, Hans-Georg: *Die Männer von U995* (Hess-Press, 1999)

Hoza, Steve, *PW: First Person Accounts of German PoWs in Arizona* (E6B Publications, 1995)

Köhl, Fritz & Niestlé, Axel: *Vom Original zum Modell: Uboottyp IXC* (Bernard & Graefe, 1990)

Vom Original zum Modell: *Uboottyp VIIC* (Bernard & Graefe, 1994)

Martienssen, Anthony: *Hitler And His Admirals* (E. P. Dutton & Co., 1949)

Merten, Karl-Friedrich: *Schicksalswaffe U-Boot* (E. S. Mittler & Sohn, 1994)

Neitzel, Sönke: *Die deutschen Ubootbunker*, (Bernard & Graefe, 1995)

Padfield, Peter: *War Beneath The Sea* (Pimlico, 1995)

Paterson, Lawrence: *The First U-Boat Flotilla* (Pen & Sword, 2002)

Paterson, Lawrence: *Hitler's Grey Wolves* (Greenhill Books, 2006)

Paterson, Lawrence: *The Second U-Boat Flotilla* (Pen & Sword, 2003)

Paterson, Lawrence: *U-Boat War Patrol* (Greenhill Books, 2004)

Paterson, Lawrence: *U-boats in the Mediterranean* (Chatham Publishing, 2007)

Paterson, Lawrence: *Weapons of Desperation* (Chatham Publishing, 2006)

Rohwer, Jürgen: *Axis Submarine Successes of World War Two* (Greenhill Books, 1999)

Rössler, Eberhard: *The U-Boat* (Arms & Armour, 1981)

Rössler, Eberhard: *Vom Original zum Modell: Uboottyp II* (Bernard & Graefe, 1999)

Schramm, Percy E. (editor): *Kriegstagebuch des OKW* (Bernard & Graefe, 2002)

Sebag-Montefiore, Hugh: *Enigma* (Weidenfield & Nicholson, 2000)

Showell, Jak Mallmann (editor): *Führer Conferences On Naval Affairs* (Greenhill Books, 2004)

Showell, Jak Mallmann: *The German Navy Handbook* (Sutton Publishing, 1999)

Showell, Jak Mallmann: *The U-boat Century* (Chatham Publishing, 2006)

Showell, Jak Mallmann: *U-Boat Command and the Battle of the Atlantic* (Conway Maritime Press, 1989)

Showell, Jak Mallmann: *U-Boat Commanders and Crews* (Crowood Press, 1998)

Showell, Jak Mallmann: *U-Boats Under The Swastika* (Ian Allen, 1987)

Stern, Robert: *Type VII U-Boats* (Brockhampton Press, 1991)

Tarrant, V.E.: *Last Year Of The Kriegsmarine* (Arms & Armour, 1994)

Trevor-Roper, Hugh: *Hitler's Table Talk* (Weidenfield & Nicholson, 1953)

Werner, Herbert: *Iron Coffins* (Henry Holt & Company, 1969)

Wetzel, Eckard: *U995. Das Uboot vor dem Marine Ehrenmal in Laboe* (Karl Müller Verlag, 1992)

Wilmot, Chester: *The Struggle For Europe* (Collins, 1952)

Winton, John (editor): *The War At Sea* (Book Club Associates, 1974)

Wynn, Kenneth: *U-Boat Operations of the Second World War, Vols 1 & 2,* (Chatham Publishing, 1997)

Picture credits

Page number and position are indicated as follows:
L = Left, TL = Top left, TR = Top right, C = Center,
CL = Center left, B = Bottom, BL = Bottom left, etc:

Author's collection:

14; 15: BR; 16: T, CL; 17: B; 21; 22: BR; 23: TR; 24: BL;
34: BL; 35: CL, CR; 37; 39: R; 40: L; 41: BL; 42: CL; 43:
CL, CR, BR; 45: TL, TR, BL; 49: 51: TL, TR; 52: TL; 53:
TR; 55: B; 56: CL, B, TR; 60: TR; 61: TL, TR, BR; 66: TR,
BR; 67: B; 69: TL, TR; 70: TL, TC, BC; 74: BL, BR; 75:
TL,; 82: BL, BR; 83: TR; 85: TR; 86: TR, C; 87: TL, TR;
88: B; 89: TR; 90: TR; 91: CR; 92: TR; 101: TL, BR; 102:
BR; 103: TR, TL, BR; 104: TR; 105: L, BC, R; 106: BC,
TR; 110: CL, TC; 116: CL; 119: TR, BL, BR; 120: BL;
122: C; 123: TR; 127: BL, BR; 134: TL, TR; 135: TL, BC;
136: TR; 141: TR; 142: CL, TR; 144: TC; CL; B; 145: TL,
TR, BR; 150: L, CT; back of jacket and cover: BL, BR.

Eric-Jan Bakker:

27: BR, TR, C; 49: TL; 71, R; 85: BR; 87: B; 93: BR; 100:
BL; 107: BR; 135: CR; 140: CT; 146: BL; 149: TR, CR,
BR.

Steve Hoza:

117: CT.

Mike Kemble:

73: BR; 132: CL, CR; 133: CL (These images were
received by Mike Kemble from members of the crews of
Walker's ships, who gave permission for them to be used
as appropriate, at Mike Kemble's discretion.)

Tom Perera/The Enigma Museum:

89: L

U-Boot Archiv:

11-12; 16: CR; 17: T; 18; 19; 22: TL, BL; 24: TL. BR; 25:
BL, BR; 26: B; 28-29; 36: BL, BR; 39: TC, BC; 41: CL;
44: BL; 50: BL; 53: BC; 58: TL, TR; 59: BL, TR; 67: TL; 68:
BL, BR; 72: TL, TC, BR; 73: TL, TR; 75: BL, BR; 84: BC;
85: BL; 91: BL, BR; 99: TR; 106: BL; 108: BL, BR; 109: TR;
120: TC, BC; 121: TR; 122: CL; 123: BR; 124: CL, BR;
136: BL, BR; 138-139; 140: BL, BR; 141: CL, BL; 142:
BC; 143: CR, BR; 147: B; 148: L; jacket, back flap;

All the *U995* interior and exterior photographs were
made aboard *U995* at Laboe, Germany by Neil
Sutherland, and are the copyright of Elephant Book
Company Ltd.

The memorabilia photographs featured in the book were
made at the Deutsches U-Boot-Museum, Cuxhaven-
Altenbruch, Germany by Neil Sutherland, and are the
copyright of Elephant Book Company Ltd.

Jacket and front cover illustration:

U-47 at Scapa Flow by Donald O'Brien, ISMP (website:
www.ismpart.com/obrien.html)

Acknowledgments

Author's acknowledgments

As always in the writing of a book such as this many people have been of great help and guidance. I would especially like to thank Horst Bredow of Altenbruch's U-Boat Archive for opening the amazing collection of artifacts and information for study and photography. Also, special thanks to Jak Mallmann Showell, not only for guiding us through the Archive's material but also for sharing his time and extensive knowledge while this book was being written. Many thanks to Dieter Seidler and the staff of the Deutscher Marinebund e.V., without whom the photographs taken aboard *U995* would not have been possible. *U995* is the last remaining Type VII U-boat in existence, and provided an excellent framework on which to structure this book.

I am deeply indebted to Eric-Jan Bakker in the Netherlands for providing some of the excellent photos that are included here (particularly those taken aboard *U281*) and of course for his detailed knowledge of the subject. Also, many thanks to Steve Hoza from Arizona for his help with material relating to *U162* and *U604*; best of luck with your museum work.

I would also like to thank Sarah for putting up with my frequent absences as I drifted off (either mentally or physically) into the subject matter of this book. Also to Will Steeds, Laura Ward, and Neil Sutherland of Elephant Books, who made this project happen.

Last, but certainly not least, I would like to extend my deepest gratitude to the many *Kriegsmarine* veterans and their families who have made me so welcome on my frequent visits to once again ask about events from so long ago. It has been a humbling experience.

Editors' acknowledgments

The editors would particularly like to thank Horst Bredow and Jak P. Mallmann Showell of the U-Boat Archive, Altenbruch, Germany for allowing us to photograph items in the museum, and for allowing us to use photographs from the Archive's collection in this book; sincere thanks, too, to Jak P. Mallmann Showell for his help and advice throughout. Particular thanks also to Dieter W. Seidler of the Deutscher Marinebund, e.V., Laboe, Germany for making us so welcome and for allowing us to photograph throughout *U995* at Laboe. Last but not least, thanks to Mike Kemble; and to Dr Tom Perera and the Enigma Museum (website: www.w1tp.com/enigma; *see also* www.antiquefirearm.com).